# TITLE II-A

# The Measurement of the Intelligence of Young Children by an Object-Fitting Test

UNIVERSITY OF MINNESOTA
THE INSTITUTE OF CHILD WELFARE
MONOGRAPH SERIES NO. V

# PLATE I

## MATERIALS FOR THE OBJECT-FITTING TEST

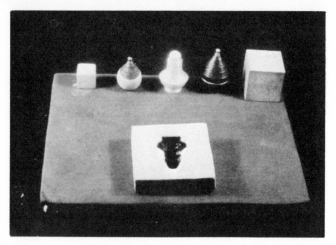

*Above.*—All the blocks and objects. *Below.*—Ready for the child's response to block 12.

# The Measurement of the Intelligence of Young Children by an Object-Fitting Test

RUTH ELLEN ATKINS, Ph. D.

FORMERLY RESEARCH ASSISTANT
INSTITUTE OF CHILD WELFARE

GREENWOOD PRESS, PUBLISHERS
WESTPORT, CONNECTICUT

Library of Congress Cataloging in Publication Data
Atkins, Ruth Ellen, 1885-
    The measurement of the intelligence of young children
by an object-fitting test.

    Reprint of the ed. published by the University of
Minnesota Press, Minneapolis, which was issued as no. 5
of the University of Minnesota, Institute of child Wel-
fare, Monograph series.
    Originally presented as the author's thesis, Univer-
sity of Minnesota, 1929.
    Bibliography:  p.
    Includes index.
    1.  Mental tests.  2.  Child Study.  I.  Title.
II.  Series:  Minnesota.  University.  Institute of
Child Development and Welfare.  Monograph series ; no. 5.
BF431.A68  1975      153.9'3       75-12673
ISBN 0-8371-8083-X

# FOREWORD

For some time there has been need of a nonverbal intelligence test for use with young children. In this monograph Dr. Atkins presents such a test, the striking characteristics of which are, first, that the material is unique and at the same time well within the experience of all young children; second, that the test can be administered without the use of language either for giving instructions or for responding and is therefore well adapted for use with young normal children, with the deaf, and with children from foreign homes; and third, that it is adequately standardized at each age level on 150 children who constitute a representative sample of the Minneapolis population. This new test is a worthy addition to the measuring instruments available for use with young children and should make possible studies of the intellectual capacity of children who are not reached effectively by the scales now in use.

The monograph is divided into two parts, the first of which describes the development and standardization of the test; the second consists of a manual for its administration. In the manual explicit directions for giving and scoring the test and norms for computing mental age are found. Percentile scores are also represented.

The materials for giving the test may be obtained from the C. H. Stoelting Company, Chicago.

JOHN E. ANDERSON,
Director, Institute of Child Welfare

# ACKNOWLEDGMENTS

To all those parents, principals, teachers, doctors, nurses, and other social workers whose generous cooperation made it possible for her to test the children in their care, yet whom it is impossible to name here because of their number, the writer is most grateful.

Her thanks are also due to Professor John E. Anderson, through whom, as director of the Institute of Child Welfare, the present investigation was financed.

Especially would she express her gratitude and sincere appreciation to the three who read the manuscript and gave constructive criticisms thereon — Professors Wilford S. Miller and John G. Rockwell of the Department of Educational Psychology, her official advisors, and Professor Florence L. Goodenough of the Institute of Child Welfare, whose clear thinking and painstaking workmanship in preschool research set the standard to which the writer endeavored to make this study approach.

RUTH E. ATKINS

# TABLE OF CONTENTS

# LIST OF TABLES

## LIST OF PLATES

# PART I

## THE DEVELOPMENT AND STANDARDIZATION OF THE OBJECT-FITTING TEST

# CHAPTER I

# THE TESTING SITUATION IN THE PRESCHOOL FIELD

## INTRODUCTION

The modern mental testing movement has apparently reached its majority, yet when one seeks to gauge the intelligence of a child under five years of age, he finds that the means are very limited and far from satisfactory. This is especially true if the subject to be tested is extremely shy, negativistic, or distractible, or if he has any language handicap, such as unwillingness or inability to talk, noncomprehension of the English language, or deafness. Since one can never be sure of the exact degree to which these disturbing factors may be operative in any given case, the most valid test would seem to be that which affords them least scope of action. Search should therefore be made in the field of nonverbal test elements.

A cursory view of preschool intelligence tests shows that they may be classified under three headings.

1. Verbal scales, such as the Binet, all contain some nonverbal elements, but the significance of these separate items is lost in the total score. A negativistic or distractible child cannot do himself justice in such an examination.

2. The so-called "performance" tests demand no verbal response from the subject, but they do assume a certain comprehension of spoken English.

3. In the strictly nonlanguage tests the child can learn by observation alone what to do with the material provided and he is in no way penalized for language difficulties.

The history of the testing movement as a whole is too well known to require a review of it here, but a consideration of Tables I and II may call attention to certain facts regarding these three types of nonlanguage test elements.

# TABLE I

## Nonverbal Elements in Verbal Intelligence Scales

| Type of Response Demanded | Year Norm | Experimenter | Date |
|---|---|---|---|
| Pointing in response to verbal direction to: | | | |
| Parts of the body | 3 | Binet (20)* | 1905 |
| Longer line | 4 | Binet (20) | 1905 |
| Similar form | 4 | Kuhlmann (20) | 1912 |
| Prettier picture | 5 | Terman (35) | 1916 |
| Larger dog | 3 | Kubo (19) | 1922 |
| Objects in pictures | 2 | Kuhlmann (20) | 1922 |
| Similar form (from memory) | 4 | Kuhlmann (20) | 1912 |
| Same color (from memory) | 4 or 5 | Kuhlmann (20) | 1920 |
| Same form (from memory) | 4 or 5 | Herderschee (13) | 1920 |
| Using pen or pencil in response to verbal direction: | | | |
| Copying a square (pen) | 5 | Binet (20) | 1908 |
| Tracing a square (pencil) | 4 | Porteus (30) | 1918 |
| Drawing a human figure (pencil) | 4 or 5 | Herderschee (13) | 1920 |
| Tracing an irregular form (pencil) | 4 | Kuhlmann (20) | 1922 |
| Copying a circle (pencil) | 2 | Kuhlmann (20) | 1922 |
| Miscellaneous nonverbal responses to verbal directions: | | | |
| Selecting heavier weight | 5 | Binet (20) | 1905 |
| Imitating simple movements | 2 | Binet (20) | 1905 |
| Obeying simple commands | 2 | Binet (20) | 1905 |
| Obeying three commands | 5 | Terman (35) | 1916 |
| Miscellaneous nonverbal responses to nonverbal stimuli: | | | |
| Removing wrapping from food | 2 | Binet (20) | 1905 |
| Putting out tongue in imitation | 3 | Herderschee (13) | 1920 |
| Shaking hands | 3 | Herderschee (13) | 1920 |
| Spitting out objectionable solid | 2 | Kuhlmann (20) | 1922 |
| Drinking from a glass | 2 | Kuhlmann (20) | 1922 |
| Feeding self with fork or spoon | 2 | Kuhlmann (20) | 1922 |

* The numbers in parentheses are references to the bibliography.

Only those scales for which norms have been proposed for children under five and one-half years of age have been listed. The author does not claim to know exactly what each of these elements tests, but she has classified them under what seems to be the most obvious factor.[1]

## NONVERBAL ELEMENTS IN VERBAL SCALES

In Table I those items in verbal scales that call for no verbal response from the child are listed under four general classifications.

1. Nine items call for "pointing" in response to verbal directions. The real test for the first six of these is that of language comprehension. In the last three, in which immediate memory of visual impressions is also tested, success depends in large part upon the child's ability to understand the verbal directions.

2 and 3. The responses of using pen or pencil in a prescribed way and of obeying other miscellaneous directions also presuppose language comprehension, especially in those tests where no demonstration of the task is allowed.

4. There remain six items that may be listed under the classification of responses to nonverbal stimuli. In these the visual stimuli are usually reenforced for the English-speaking child by verbal directions more or less perfectly understood. Thus, even with these nonverbal elements in verbal scales the child who does not comprehend spoken English is at a disadvantage.

## NONVERBAL ELEMENTS FOR WHICH SEPARATE NORMS HAVE BEEN PROPOSED

There are at least eight general types of response called for in the test elements listed in Table II. The most frequent is that of fitting a block into a recess, the number of

[1] As Thorndike has said, "We measure the available power of intellectual achievement without any specification as to its genesis . . . nothing about the causation of the abilities measured" (see No. 36 in the bibliography, p. 95).

recesses presented to the child at one time varying from one to eighteen. Table II is to be read as follows. The Goddard Form Board Test calls for the response of "fitting in," and consists of ten blocks and ten recesses. Goddard (No. 8 in the bibliography) first proposed a norm for two-year-olds based on six cases. He gives no description (section B of this table) of his method of selecting subjects. The Healy Picture Completion Test, which belongs to this general type, is different from the others in that any of its sixty blocks will fit any of the ten openings. The child must, therefore, comprehend not only the examiner's instructions, which tell him to select the one best block, but also the relationships shown in the picture, and he must then make each of the proper selections from the sixty blocks presented.

Next in frequency is the type of test demanding the fitting of several blocks together to fill a single recess. These blocks may be all alike or may be of extremely different sizes and shapes; they may bear pictures or be of plain wood. The number of blocks to be fitted into one recess ranges from two to sixteen, and from one to four of the recesses may be presented to the child at once.

Somewhat similar but simpler are those tests of the puzzle-picture type that merely require the fitting together of several parts of a dissected picture presented to the child without any containing frame. The manikin tests may also be placed in this class, although the use of different material perhaps alters the problem somewhat. Piling blocks according to a model constructed while the child watches and building the "Little Pink Tower" after seeing it built once and then knocked down demand similar motor responses. The latter test also involves the use of memory. Putting a button through a buttonhole is certainly somewhat similar to fitting a block into a recess, yet this test probably requires more manipulative skill because of the flexible nature of the material. Finding one's way through a maze is essentially a learning problem in which the motor abilities needed are determined by the type of maze. Matching colors or forms

## TABLE II

NONVERBAL ELEMENTS WITH SEPARATE NORMS USED IN
PRESCHOOL TESTS

SECTION A. DATA RELATING TO THE TESTS

| TEST MATERIAL | EXPERIMENTER | LOWEST YEAR FOR WHICH DATA IS PRESENTED | SCORING METHOD |
|---|---|---|---|
| RESPONSE OF " FITTING IN " | | | |
| Goddard Form Board (10 blocks, 10 recesses) | Goddard (8)* | 2 | Average time of three trials |
| | Pintner and Paterson (29) | 5 | Shortest time of three trials |
| | Wallin (37) | 4 | Average time of three trials |
| | Herrick (14) | 5 | Shortest time of three trials |
| | Sylvester (33) | 1¾ | Time |
| Witmer Form Board (11 blocks, 11 recesses) | Young (42) | 4 | Shortest time of three trials |
| | Young and Young (43) | 4 | Time of first trial |
| | Ide (16) | 4 | Time of first trial |
| Adaptation (1 block, 1 recess) | Pintner and Paterson (29) | 4 | Number of correct moves |
| Three-Figure Form Board (3 blocks, 3 recesses) | Hallowell (11) | 1½ | Success in learning or in completion |
| Three-Disc Form Board (3 blocks, 3 recesses) | Hallowell (11) | 1½ | Success in learning or in completion |

* The numbers in parentheses are references to the bibliography.

## TABLE II—*Continued*

| Test Material | Experimenter | Lowest Year for Which Data Is Presented | Scoring Method |
|---|---|---|---|
| RESPONSE OF "FITTING IN" — *Continued* | | | |
| Form Board 1A (3 blocks, 3 recesses) | Dearborn, Shaw, and Lincoln (6) | 5 | Time and moves in combined score |
| Five-Figure Form Board (5 blocks, 5 recesses) | Johnson (17) | 3 | Time |
| Nest of Cubes (4 blocks, 4 recesses) | Stutsman (32) | 1½ | Time |
| Mare and Foal (7 blocks, 7 recesses) | Pintner and Paterson (29) | 5 | Time and number of errors |
| | Stutsman (32) | 3 | Time |
| | Johnson (17) | 2½ | Time |
| Peg Form Board A and B (6 pegs, 6 recesses for each) | Wallin (38) | 1¾ | Time |
| | Stutsman (32) | 1½ | Time |
| | Goodenough (9) | 1¾ | Time |
| Montessori Cylinders, A, B, C (6 blocks, 6 recesses for each) | Woolley (39) | 3–3¾ | Time |
| Witmer Cylinders (18 blocks, 18 recesses) | Johnson (17) | 3 | Time |
| Picture completion (60 blocks, 10 recesses) | Pintner and Anderson (26) | 5 | Point score |
| RESPONSE OF "FITTING IN TOGETHER" | | | |
| Sixteen Cubes (16 blocks, 1 recess) | Stutsman (32) | 1½ | Time and number correct |
| Gwyn Triangle (4 blocks, 2 recesses) | Pintner and Paterson (29) | 4 | Time and number of errors |

TABLE II—*Continued*

| TEST MATERIAL | EXPERIMENTER | LOWEST YEAR FOR WHICH DATA IS PRESENTED | SCORING METHOD |
|---|---|---|---|
| RESPONSE OF "FITTING IN TOGETHER" — *Continued* | | | |
| Two-Figure Form Board (9 blocks, 2 recesses) | Pintner and Paterson (29) | 4 | Time and number of moves |
| | Johnson (17) | 4 | Time |
| Casuist Form Board (12 blocks, 4 recesses) | Pintner and Paterson (29) | 4 | Time and number of errors |
| | Johnson (17) | 3 | Time |
| Hollow Square (3–4 blocks, 1 recess) | Lincoln (22) | 2½ | Total time |
| Glueck Ship (10 blocks, 1 recess) | Pintner and Paterson (29) | 5 | Point score |
| RESPONSE OF "FITTING TOGETHER" | | | |
| Puzzle Picture I | Stutsman (32) | 2½ | Time |
| II | Stutsman (32) | 3½ | Time |
| III | Stutsman (32) | 3½ | Time |
| Manikin | Pintner and Paterson (29) | 2 | Point score |
| | Johnson (17) | 2½ | Point score |
| | Stutsman (32) | 3½ | Point score |
| Dissected Picture | Johnson (17) | 2½ | Point score |
| RESPONSE OF "BUILDING UP" | | | |
| Little Pink Tower (5 blocks) | Woolley (39) | 3 | Time |
| | Stutsman (32) | 2½ | Time |
| Three-Cube Pyramid (3 blocks) | Stutsman (32) | 2½ | Time |
| Six-Cube Pyramid | Stutsman (32) | 3 | Time |

## TABLE II—*Continued*

| Test Material | Experimenter | Lowest Year for Which Data Is Presented | Scoring Method |
|---|---|---|---|
| RESPONSE OF " FINDING A WAY THROUGH " | | | |
| Slot Maze A | Young (40) | 4 | Time of first trial |
| RESPONSE OF " SELECTING SIMILAR " | | | |
| Color Matching | Hallowell (11) | 1½ | Success, partial success, and failure |
| Color and Form | Dearborn, Anderson, and Christianson (5) | 4–5 | Time |
| RESPONSE OF "PUTTING BUTTON THROUGH BUTTONHOLE " | | | |
| One-Button | Stutsman (32) | 1½ | Time |
| Two-Button | Stutsman (32) | 2½ | Time |
| Four-Button | Stutsman (32) | 3 | Time |
| RESPONSE OF " TAPPING IN IMITATION " | | | |
| Knox Cube | Pintner and Paterson (25) | 4 | Point score |
| | Pintner and Paterson (29) | 3 | Point score |
| | Johnson (17) | 3 | Point score |

## TABLE II—*Continued*

SECTION B. SUBJECTS ON WHICH NONVERBAL TEST NORMS ARE BASED

(All that could be learned as to each experimenter's sampling method has been given below in section B. This division was made to simplify the table.)

| EXPERIMENTER | DESCRIPTION OF ENTIRE SAMPLING |
|---|---|
| Goddard (8) | None. |
| Pintner and Paterson (29) | From upper and lower middle-class public schools, Columbus, Ohio. |
| Wallin (37) | 75 per cent of average intelligence, 12½ per cent bright, and 12½ per cent dull; from public schools in Philadelphia. |
| Herrick (14) | Unselected Panchanas and Brahmans from two schools in southern India. |
| Sylvester (33) | None. |
| Young (42) | All in the regular classes of the public schools of Philadelphia; of poorer foreign and American professional parentage. |
| Ide (16) | Philadelphia kindergarten children from homes of Americans well able to provide but not professional, foreigners well above the poverty level, and a few charity cases. |
| Hallowell (11) | 25 per cent of high intelligence level, 11 per cent from well-clinics, 23 per cent from day nurseries, 30 per cent from child-placing agencies, and 11 per cent from institutions; 85 per cent whites, 15 per cent negroes. |
| Dearborn, Shaw, and Lincoln (6) | None. |

TABLE II — *Concluded*

| EXPERIMENTER | DESCRIPTION OF ENTIRE SAMPLING |
|---|---|
| Johnson (17) | From the City and Country School and other private schools of New York; rated very superior in Stanford-Binet. |
| Stutsman (32) | 39.7 per cent from better homes on the Merrill Palmer waiting list, 35.5 per cent from mediocre homes through public kindergartens, 16.2 per cent from orphanages, day nurseries, and child care agencies, and 8.6 per cent from baby health clinics. |
| Wallin (38) | From baby contests and institutions. |
| Goodenough (9) | A very careful selection on basis of paternal occupation to constitute a representative sampling of the Minneapolis population according to census returns. |
| Woolley (39) | From Merrill Palmer waiting list, kindergartens, nurseries, and public schools. |
| Pintner and Anderson (26) | From two schools of better class, one of middle class, one of poorer class. |
| Lincoln (22) | From hospitals, private schools, and habit clinics. |
| Young (40) | All from four public schools, two average, one above average, and one below average. |
| Dearborn, Anderson, and Christiansen (5) | None. |
| Pintner and Paterson (25) | From kindergartens, nurseries, and settlements in Columbus, Ohio; known feebleminded not included. |

requires no comprehension of verbal directions if the process is clearly demonstrated by a fore-exercise. The Knox Cube Test is unique in its requirements, and very careful attention to the examiner's performance and immediate memory of it are necessary for success.[2]

## TEN CRITERIA OF A GOOD TEST FOR YOUNG CHILDREN

1. *Intrinsic interest in the material.* — The results of the test can be considered an adequate measure of ability only when whole-hearted effort has been put forth by the child, for anything less produces only indeterminate responses. Urging, indiscriminate praising, and all other forms of extrinsic motivation so commonly used with older children in the endeavor to keep them up to maximum effort are of much less avail with the younger child. When such inducements are used, they generally leave the investigator in doubt as to the reliability of the test results. The only thing the tester can say with assurance is that the child has at least as much ability as his test results indicate.

If the child's attention is diverted in any way — by emotional reaction, voluntary opposition, or by some outer distraction — the stimuli of the test fail to evoke genuine responses. It is comparatively easy to conduct the examination of a docile child who is interested and eager to do his best. It is the shy, distractible, or negativistic child who is a problem. Any factor that helps to transform this child into the opposite type, at least for the duration of the test, is an asset. Intrinsic interest in the material is such a factor, and the first requirement of a test suitable for the young child is that it make a genuine appeal to his interest.

2. *Minimum of oral directions.* — Tests calling for verbal responses are, as a whole, less interesting to young children than are the so-called "performance" tests. Certain types of examining instructions frequently excite nega-

[2] Gesell distinctly states of his work, "No attempt was made by statistical methods to consolidate the items into a delimited and inflexible psychometric scale. . . . Our purpose has been to devise an adjustable clinical instrument. . . . It is not presumed that these normative items always bear a significant relation to so-called general intelligence" (7, p. 5). For this reason no items from his list are included in Table II.

tivism. The child may recognize a command heard at home or one with which he perhaps has associated a negative affect, such as instructions to "Point," "Say," "Tell me," "Look, do just as I do" (see Goodenough, 10, pp. 74, 75, 77, 89). It is often difficult to camouflage commands sufficiently to keep up the play spirit so essential to whole-hearted response, and consequently the child often balks. Even if he seems to comply with the request he generally does so in a manner that plainly betrays his lack of interest.

The shy child, however, is the one most apt to receive a lower rating than he deserves. Although he usually seems docile and perhaps appears to respond, yet he may be so inhibited by fear as to be incapable of revealing his true ability. Only through practice does an examiner learn to recognize these cases and to allow adequate time for the fear to wear off before beginning a test. In the writer's experience this timidity is found more frequently in children from the lower social classes, and it can usually be overcome to some extent by sufficient play before the test, by making the toys prominent and the examination inconspicuous, and by avoiding conversational demands — especially with children from non-English-speaking homes. It is difficult for an adult to realize how terrifying she and her queer jargon may be to a foreign child who has seen but few strangers or who has seldom been away from a family whose language he understands. A good test for these children, therefore, requires only a minimum of oral direction and gives a maximum of prominence to intriguing play material.

3. *Briefness of required attention span.* — a. The attention of the *very young child* is so variable that it is impossible to hold him to a single task for a long time. The briefer the span of attention required by a test element, the better are the results obtained.

b. The writer has found the *extremely distractible child* most frequently among the higher social classes. With a child of this type the attention flits from object to object almost momentarily, and any test demanding sustained effort is certain of failure. A good test for the distractible child is one that employs material that constantly catches his attention by its novelty, that requires but a few seconds of attention at a time, and that gives him something to do constantly, so that he will not dissipate his energies in miscellaneous activities.

4. *Noncomplexity of materials.* — The young child can perceive but few objects at once, and complex material merely tends to confuse him and to induce chance responses. Moreover, the simpler the material the more easily it may be carried from place to place and adapted to use in the child's natural environment, where he feels most at ease.

5. *Equality of previous experience.* — Perfect achievement of this ideal is impossible, but it may be approached on the one hand by the use of very common objects familiar to most children and, on the other hand, by the presentation of a situation certain to be new to every child tested. Using a fore-exercise and allowing more than one trial at a task are two means of equalizing practice.

6. *Noncommunicability.* — Since the young child as a rule has had comparatively little experience with strangers, he is often put at a disadvantage emotionally if forced to be alone with the examiner. The presence of his mother or of an older brother or sister puts him at his ease, and he plays happily with the test material. If the material is of such a nature as to make "coaching" both during the test and before the retest impossible, the child's peace of mind may be secured with gain, rather than loss, to the validity and reliability of the results. Noncommunicability is also a distinct advantage where each of a group of children who play together is to be examined.

7. *Credit for each actual response.* — Any arbitrary decision that two out of three responses or all ten must be correct to secure any credit penalizes the child with marginal ability. It would seem that the one who has nine successes out of ten chances is surely different from the one

who has but one out of ten. For this reason the point scale has been advocated as preferable to the earlier age-level scale.

8. *Objectivity in giving and scoring.* — The directions to the examiner should be so simple that they can be easily followed and so definite that there can be no question between two examiners as to the proper procedure. The arrangement of the material and the scoring blank should be such that the examiner is free to devote practically her entire attention to the child and still be able to keep an objective record of every response.

9. *Adequate standardization.* — a. Each separate group treated in the data should be equally *representative* of the general population in regard to sex, social status, and race, since the effect of differences in these respects is still undetermined.

b. We are justified in the conclusion that we have an *adequate sampling* only when the addition of further cases does not significantly change the means of the groups. An arbitrary standard of ten, twenty-five, fifty, or a thousand cases per group will not do.

c. *Reliability* is a third requirement of standardization. A test element that is not consistent with itself or that frequently gives contradictory results on different occasions cannot be truly said to measure anything, unless it be the credulity of the examiner.

d. A test should also be *discriminative*. All the data on the curve of growth tend to show that its acceleration is most rapid during the first years of life. A month during this period may be as significant as six months or even six years later on. A valid test for young children will therefore show a relatively steady month-by-month increase in average score, and the differences between the means for various years will be statistically significant.

e. Finally, *validity* is a criterion of adequate standardization. However reliable and discriminative a test may be, it should not be called an intelligence test unless it has been checked with one or more commonly accepted criteria of general intelligence. Otherwise it may be merely a very good measure of some special ability unrelated to intellect.

10. *Complete presentation of data.*—In order that a test may be of the greatest use, it should be easily subject to further experimentation. This is possible only if all the data regarding it are available, so that another person may repeat the work exactly or may carry on further experimentation. If these complete data cannot be published, there should at least be a reference stating that they exist and where they may be found.

### CRITICISM OF AVAILABLE TEST ELEMENTS

If these are the criteria of a good test for young children, how are they met by the available test elements? In spite of their evident strong points the materials listed in Table II call for adverse criticism under the three heads of (1) standardization technique, (2) presentation of data, and (3) influence of extraneous factors.

1. *Standardization technique.*—Whether success in making any of the types of objective response called for in the available tests is highly correlated with mental ability or whether a child would make the same response upon a repetition of the test are problems as yet practically untouched. Inadequate standardization is also evidenced by the small number of cases on which norms for each age level are based. Some of the norms proposed are based on only five or six cases, and occasionally even one child tested at a given age has been considered sufficient to suggest a standard.

Frequently no attempt, or else a very inadequate one, has been made to secure a representative sampling. Either the extremes of occupational status alone are represented, or they are omitted entirely and only the middle class is included. Still more frequently no clear statement regarding social class is made. The number of boys and girls has not been kept constant, yet several investigators have claimed to find sex differences in response. The one test (the Wallin Peg Form Board) for which norms have been obtained upon an adequate representative sampling at each age level shows a self-reliability of .32 to .72 and a correlation with an outside criterion of .28 to .48. These coefficients are scarcely high enough to justify its use alone as a test of general mental ability. No other test element has been satisfactorily checked—either with an outside criterion of validity or with itself for self-reliability. Since Woolley's reliability coefficients are based on from twenty to twenty-five children ranging in age from three to six years, it is not surprising that she finds a higher correlation with chronological than with mental age. Her correlation coefficients in no way prove the validity of the Montessori Cylinders as an intelligence test.

As might be expected from such technique, norms obtained by different experimenters with the same material do not agree. The classification of a child depends upon which norms the examiner uses. Goodenough's work on the Wallin Peg Form Board has set a standard for future work in this field, and it is to be hoped that other early test elements may soon receive the same careful treatment.

2. *Presentation of data.*—Frequently authors have presented the data so incompletely that it is impossible to determine what was actually accomplished. The materials for the various tests are not standardized, and the same names are applied to materials that are different in details although they are of the same general type. Norms established with the Goddard and Sylvester Form Board are sometimes used with the Witmer; the Rossolimo Pictures used by Johnson are not those used by Rossolimo himself.

Age groups are not accurately described. "Two-year-olds" may mean children aged from one year and six months to two years, five months, and thirty days; or from one year, eleven months, and sixteen days to two years, eleven months, and fifteen days; or from two years to two years, eleven months, and thirty days.

A correlation coefficient may have been computed on the age range of a single year or on a range extending over several years. Almost never are the standard deviations of the distributions stated. The sex, nationality, and social status of the populations upon which norms are reported have also been insufficiently described in many cases. When a fairly good description of the complete population has been given, there is too often no data on the constitution of the sample for each separate year. It is therefore possible that the majority of the two-year-olds were from the professional classes and the majority of the four-year-olds from the laboring classes. Such selection may tend to invalidate any norms secured. Even Bronner does not seem to have considered this factor.

Furthermore, there is no generally accepted policy in dealing with the scores of non-cooperative children. Some examiners include all but very negativistic cases in their data; others exclude all about which there is any doubt; still others make no statement regarding such cases.

3. *Influence of extraneous factors.*— Certain extraneous factors militate against obtaining a true mental rating with any of these tests. These are (a) personality, (b) chance, (c) unequal practice, (d) speed of reaction, and (e) language ability.

a. As a rule the materials used in the tests of Table II have high intrinsic interest (see Bridges, 3). Their presentation seldom arouses the negativism so near the surface at these ages (see Levy, 21). But, as stated above, when the problem is complicated by many parts or requires several minutes for its solution, the young child tends to weary of it and must be urged to continue. The test then becomes one of docility and perseverance, not one of mental ability.

b. Chance operates most strongly in those tests where several blocks must be fitted in together or where the material is not self-corrective. From the profusion of parts before him the child may by chance make an early selection placement that effectively prevents any speedy solution of the problem. This is true, for example, with the Wallin Peg Form Board, C and D, and is probably responsible in a large measure for its low reliability.

c. It is generally conceded that individuals may be justly

compared as to their performance in any given test only when their familiarity with the material used in it is approximately equal. Both Little Pink Tower and the Nest of Cubes contain material that is a familiar part of the environment of many children but that may present a practically new situation to others. This invalidates their use as mental tests unless they are included in a scale of so many diverse items that these differences in experience are largely equalized.

d. The most common method of scoring the tests listed in Table II is that of time in seconds, probably because it is an objective and very simple procedure. Thorndike, however, states that "it seems unwise to attach much weight to speed in intelligence examinations in general" (36, p. 400). He found correlations of only .29 between rate of speed and age level. Speed is probably especially inadequate as an indication of mental level in the young child, since his fluctuating attention and his tendency to stop and play with the materials may run up the time score out of all proportion to his actual mental inability. Thorndike points out that "nothing useful concerning an ability is measured by the time required to fail at a task" (36, p. 482), and in all but the single-block, single-recess type of test the time score is an inseparable compound of times of successful and unsuccessful placements.

e. As has been pointed out above, the ability to comprehend spoken English plays some part in determining the score for every one of the test elements listed. The oral vocabulary requirements for the verbal directions used in the nonlanguage tests of Table II range from 7 or 8 words in a simple command for the form boards to 50 words in complex-compound sentences in the directions for the Picture Completion Test. These may seem very small requirements, but when one remembers that there is no evidence that the language ability of the young child is highly correlated with intelligence, the unfairness of such tests is apparent.

Arthur found that "on the second exposure of the word

'crescent' or 'triangle,' the child would point to the correct form, while it might take fifteen or twenty repetitions before he could name the word" (2, p. 263).

In twenty-six of the early published vocabularies of two-year-olds there is a range of from 5 to 1,227 words (see Table III). The child with the smallest vocabulary is a daughter of Margaret Morse Nice (24). At two years her vocabulary consisted of but 5 words, and even at three she had only 48 words at her command. Her later development, however, showed that she was in no way mentally

TABLE III

ORAL VOCABULARIES OF TWENTY-SIX TWO-YEAR-OLDS

| NUMBER OF CASES | NUMBER OF WORDS REPORTED | NUMBER OF CASES | NUMBER OF WORDS REPORTED |
|---|---|---|---|
| 3 | 0–49 | 1 | 500–549 |
| 0 | 50–99 | 1 | 550–599 |
| 2 | 100–149 | 1 | 600–649 |
| 0 | 150–199 | 1 | 650–699 |
| 0 | 200–249 | 3 | 700–749 |
| 2 | 250–299 | 2 | 750–799 |
| 1 | 300–349 | 0 | 800–1,099 |
| 1 | 350–399 | 1 | 1,100–1,149 |
| 4 | 400–449 | 0 | 1,150–1,199 |
| 3 | 450–499 | 1 | 1,200–1,249 |

subnormal, for at four years her vocabulary included 1,135 words. Yet consider how she would have compared on any language test at the age of two with the large number of two-year-olds having vocabularies of over 700 words. There are doubtless many more cases of small vocabularies than appear here, since the natural tendency of fond parents is to report only those children who have phenomenally high records. Smith states that her vocabulary test "proved inapplicable" to children as young as two and one-half years "unless they were of superior mental ability" (31, pp. 30, 53). She used but three cases at this age.

It may be urged that comprehension of all the words

in the verbal directions is not essential to success in the test. If so, why are the words used? If a child is as likely to work at maximum speed and to make a good score without being told to do the task "as quickly and with as few errors as possible," why give the direction? Is it not more probable that the degree to which he does grasp the meaning of the words is reflected in his final score?

## Special Needs for Nonlanguage Tests

Even if language ability were perfectly correlated with intelligence in the normal English-speaking child, the available tests would still be inadequate for use with deaf children or those with a foreign language handicap. Yet many of the tests included in Table II have been used in attempts to determine general intelligence, and conclusions of vital importance have been drawn from them.

The three types of young children who are especially handicapped by present methods are the deaf child, the child from a foreign home who knows little or no English, and the normal child who is slow in language development, all of whom are heavily penalized by any existing test. For the deaf even more than for the hearing child an early determination of mental ability is of utmost importance. Seventy-four per cent of the deaf reported in the 1910 census became deaf before their fifth year. A small number of these have taken their places in society with almost no apparent handicap. They read speech from the lips of their fellows and are able to speak intelligibly in reply. Why have the vast majority lagged far behind this ideal, stigmatized as "deaf and dumb" and shut off from fellowship with their equals? Perhaps it is because the attainment of this ideal ability is dependent upon two conditions, average native intelligence and an early opportunity for oral training. Lowry states that "without a fair share of intellect, speech can never be mastered by the deaf" (23, p. 1090). Pintner and Paterson report that "ability to profit by the oral method correlates rather highly with general mental ability" (28, p. 595) and that "the normal deaf child is, during his school life, about three years retarded as contrasted with the hearing child" (28, p. 210). Does this prove that the deaf child who is otherwise normal has an innate mental deficiency of three years? By no means. Words are commonly called the tools of thought. As Lowry says, "a word is the means whereby an idea can be isolated so that it can be examined. We constantly ignore things in our environment for which we have no names, such as certain trees, birds, plants, forms of clouds, and as constantly notice them, think about them, when once they are named for us" (23, p. 1088). The deaf child, regardless of native brightness, has little opportunity to acquire these tools of thought. The normal child is learning words throughout most of his waking moments for at least five years before his entrance into school. During these years the deaf child's vocabulary is ordinarily left to stagnate, or at best he is given a few brief hours of teaching per week. When he enters school, if he appears dull, either because of fear or lack of opportunity to learn to think, he may never be given a chance in the speech classes. Speech training for the deaf is such an individual, and therefore such a costly, process that many institutions are unable to give it to all the deaf children in their care. Because of the lack of any adequate test the favored pupils are selected on a basis of subjective judgments or poorly standardized performance tests. Thus a handicapped child who might easily have shown his ability if given a fair examination may lose his chance to take a place in the world as a normal individual.

The child who knows no English or who is retarded in speech development risks the loss of his chance in life only in case he is a subject for adoption. A poor showing then in whatever test is given him may mean missing a good home with intelligent foster parents.

The child with retarded speech development may also

become a behavior problem and, if so, needs an adequate mental examination (see Young, 41, and Healy, 12).

## STATEMENT OF THE PROBLEM

In view of the above facts it was the purpose of this study to construct and standardize an intelligence test that would meet the criteria and special needs that have been discussed. The test should, so far as possible, have intrinsic interest for young children; be administrable without oral directions; require a very brief attention span; and use simple, easily portable material with which all children have had equal experience. It should be noncommunicable. It should allow partial credit for partial success, to be determined from an objective record of the actual responses. It should be accompanied by norms based upon an adequate representative sampling of the population and by a complete presentation of the data as to reliability, discriminative capacity, and correlation with an outside criterion of validity. It should give the deaf child, the foreign-speaking child, and the child with retarded speech development an equal chance with the English-speaking child of equal mentality, and it should be equally applicable to all young children.

## SUMMARY

1. Many varieties of nonverbal test elements have been employed in the past.

2. With one exception they are inadequately standardized.

3. With the same exception the published data regarding them are incomplete.

4. They are all subject to the influence of extraneous factors that greatly decrease their validity as measures of general intelligence.

5. Lack of an accurate determination of mental ability at an early age may seriously handicap a child who is deaf,

one who becomes a subject for adoption, or one who is brought to a clinic as a behavior problem.

6. The available tests are not adequate for drawing conclusions as to innate differences between children of different races, sex, or social status, or as to the relative importance of nature and nurture.

7. The present study is an attempt to provide an intelligence test that will present equal opportunities for success to all young children of equal intellectual ability.

# CHAPTER II

# THE ORIGIN AND CONSTRUCTION OF THE TEST

## GENESIS OF THE STUDY

*Interest in nonlanguage tests.* — The writer first saw the need for a test of this sort while teaching in southeastern Asia. Those in charge of school work in Malaya are almost continually faced with the question of adoption. Children of all ages are brought to the schools, and the authorities are besought to take complete charge of them. Some of the children who were brought to the schools when very young and supported by American mission and British government funds have become brilliant students and teachers; others with the same care and training have never developed beyond a mentality of six years and have become a burden rather than a help to the educational work. Some means of determining, at least roughly, the innate abilities of children under school age would have prevented such misuse of money and effort.

But to be of use in cosmopolitan Malaya a test must necessarily be applicable without the use of language. Children are sent to school who know no language save their own Tamil, Malay, Bengalese, Fuchau, Cantonese, Japanese, Tetchiew, Hokkien, Hakka, Mandarin, English, Hinghua, Burmese, Siamese, or what not. The writer well remembers one entering class of twenty pupils in which there were representatives of eight home language groups; and many other language groups were represented in other classes. All were taught English, and what little experimentation the writer was able to do later with a modified Stanford-Binet test revealed no racial differences in intelligence but great differences between individuals of the same race. Were there innate racial differences that could have been discovered before the common experience of English schooling?

*Interest in tests for the preschool deaf child.*— Certain work on an analysis of the phonetic elements of a basal reading vocabulary brought a fuller realization of the unfortunate condition of the deaf child who loses at least three years out of his vocabulary-acquiring life and sometimes his entire chance at normal association with his fellows through lack of speech-reading instruction (see Chapter I).

## SOURCE OF THE MATERIALS USED

*Perception studies.*— In 1924–25 the writer was engaged in an experimental study of perception under the direction of John Rockwell. There were three parts to this study: (1) a learning experiment with an adaptation of the Goddard Form Board, (2) a preliminary study with ten recessed blocks, and (3) the main study with seventy-two other blocks. Some of these blocks were made of plaster and some of paper pulp. Although they were of various sizes and shapes, all were molded directly from such common objects as clothespins, bottles, boxes, bowls, and spools.[1] The method of procedure, which was somewhat similar in all three perception studies, was to place several objects and one block before the child, tell him to put in "the one that fits best," and record his first response and the time. Certain patterns of response soon made themselves evident, and as the writer watched the reactions of the children day after day, she became convinced that, although the time score was determined largely by personality traits and by the degree of motor coordination possessed by the child, the types of errors made were determined by his degree of mental development. Was it possible that here was the foundation of a nonlanguage intelligence test?

*Advantages of the perception material.*— Judged by most of the recognized criteria for such a test the material ranked high. (1) It was intrinsically very interesting to the child. (2) It required a very brief attention span, since its prob-

[1] A general idea of the objects may be gained by reference to the frontispiece and to Plate II, both of which show the material later used in the Object-Fitting Test.

lems could be presented at varying intervals. (3) It presented a situation equally new to every child, although the material used consisted of objects familiar to the daily environment of the child. (4) It was noncommunicable. (5) It permitted very objective scoring. (6) It proved to be fairly reliable when given again seven days later. (7) A correlation coefficient of .85 was found to exist between the number of correct responses in this test and a Kuhlmann-Binet or Stanford-Binet *IQ*.[2]

*Disadvantages of the perception material.*— As developed and used in the perception study the material was ill adapted for use as a nonlanguage intelligence test in the following respects. (1) It required verbal directions. (2) The large number of blocks made it extremely bulky and cumbersome. (3) It required a large, special table for its presentation. (4) It was too long and monontonous for children below the age of three years. (5) Too many objects were placed before the child at once, so that the responses of the younger children were determined largely by chance. (6) Some blocks were so poorly made that errors of response were almost inevitable. (7) Some of the blocks called for such complicated responses that no record of the errors could be kept.

Whether the material was really valid as a test of intelligence, whether it would stand an adequate check-up against a good verbal test, and whether its self-reliability was real or apparent were matters that could be determined only by a study designed for that purpose alone.

## Problems Incurred in the Preliminary Construction of the Test

Certain decisions were necessary before the experiment proper could be undertaken.

1. *Use as a measure of general intelligence.*— Could material primarily designed to study the genetic growth of per-

[2] This was over a range of four years and five months and was in part due to chronological age.

ception adequately measure general intelligence? Did success with this type of material call for all the abilities included in that term? Checked against Binet's early basic definition of intelligence and against the composite proposed by Herring, the material seemed adequate, and it was therefore decided that it was worth a trial as the foundation of an intelligence test.

| DEFINITIONS OF GENERAL INTELLIGENCE | EXEMPLIFICATION IN THE OBJECT-FITTING MATERIAL |
|---|---|

### BINET (35, p. 45)

| | |
|---|---|
| Ability to take and maintain a given direction. | Discovery that the objects will fit into the blocks and persistent attempts to fit them. |
| Ability to make adaptations for the purpose of attaining a desired end. | The turning of an object or choice of another to secure a perfect fit. |
| Power of auto-criticism. | Recognition that an object does or does not fit; leaving in place one that does and removing one that does not. |

### HERRING (15, p. 509)

| | |
|---|---|
| A conscious biological response to a stimulus resulting in environmental readjustment. | The child chooses and fits an object into the recessed block by: (1) removing an incorrect object and substituting another; (2) turning a correct object from an incorrect position; (3) leaving the correct object in a correct position. |
| By conscious solution of a problem. | No one who has seen even a tiny child absorbed in the manipulation of this material has failed to realize that it presents a series of genuine problems to him. |
| Not before solved by the same individual. | No child has had any opportunity to meet exactly these problems before, since the blocks are unique and were constructed especially for this study. |

*Number of forms.*—Should the material be arranged as a single examination or should there be two forms of approximately equal difficulty? In working with young children it is appreciably easier to obtain a large number of single records by testing each child once than to secure the same number of records from half the number of children by testing each of them twice, because minor illnesses of the child or the home duties of the mother often prevent a retest. The difficulty of making a second appointment is even greater if a fixed time interval must be maintained between the tests.

On the other hand, there were certain advantages to be gained from retesting with an alternative form. Since each child would receive two tests, it would not be necessary to locate so many children in order to obtain the same number of records. The self-reliability of the test could be determined by comparing the results of the two forms. The comparative value of the individual blocks could be checked by the reliability of responses from test to test.

It was decided that two forms should be assembled, each element of one form matching an element in the other as nearly equal to it in value as previous experience with the perception material would permit, and that these selected elements should be checked by the responses in the new experiment.

*Length of tests.*—Should one use as much or as little of the perception material as possible? Should the new test require a long or a short period of time for its administration? The general attitude has been that the longer an examination the more reliable it is. This, of course, presupposes that all the items of the test are of approximately equal reliability and validity. Kuhlmann has pointed out that a few truly discriminative test items may give as valuable results as a number of indifferent ones (20, p. 24).

A closer examination of the perception experiment data showed that some of the blocks were contributing absolutely nothing to the apparent correlation with the Binet *IQ*'s.

By a careful selection of blocks and by giving partial credit to error responses with a high discriminative value the same correlation coefficient was obtained with the use of only eight blocks.[3]

The brevity of the young child's attention span has been mentioned in Chapter I, page 14. As Bridges states, "the length of time a three-year-old's interest in an occupation usually lasts is about eight minutes. . . . We must expect children of this age to want to do something different every five or ten minutes" (3, p. 423). Since it was desirable that the new test hold the attention of children even younger than three years, it was decided to curtail the test as much as it was possible to do without appreciably lowering its reliability or validity.

*Elimination of blocks.*—After this decision the next question naturally was, what shall be eliminated and what shall be kept?

A total of eighty-four blocks had been constructed and ninety separate objects used. From these the writer selected, on the basis of high discriminative value, small size, and possibility for unequivocal scoring, the twenty blocks that seemed most promising material for a test. The size of the individual blocks was reduced by one-half. The maximum number of objects to be presented at one time was reduced to five, and the total number to twenty-two. The blocks in-

[3] These early coefficients were based on tests of only seventy-two children who ranged in age from two years and two months to six years and three months. The single intelligence quotients were roughly determined from the Stanford-Binet and Kuhlmann-Binet tests given by four examiners at widely separated intervals. The coefficients could therefore be considered merely suggestive as to the ultimate value of the material as a measure of intelligence. But the fact that the apparent correlation was probably due to some actual correlation between mental ability and response to the material and not to mere chronological age was evidenced by certain cases of equal chronological age with widely differing intelligence quotients and by other cases of differing chronological age and equal *IQ*. A distinct correspondence could be traced between results from the two types of material, but the cases were too few to constitute actual proof.

cluded in this preliminary selection, but discarded later for reasons given in Chapter III, were B6, pencil on end; A6, inverted cup; A7, small cylinder; B7, inverted bowl; A14, large top; B14, inverted salt shaker. All the objects and the blocks finally selected are shown in the frontispiece. A more complete description of these materials may be found in Part II, the manual for the administration of the Object-Fitting Test.

*No conversation.*— How could the test be made strictly nonlanguage? How could the child know what was expected of him? Would not the English-speaking child be handicapped by an atmosphere of utter silence? The use of a fore-exercise in which the child would be taught by demonstration the possibilities of the material solved the first difficulty. The ability to discover what can be done with the material evidences an ability to abstract a general rule from concrete situations, and a child who could go through the fore-exercise activities (see Part II, page 75) without perceiving the problem and developing a "set" toward fitting an object into the recess would be below the mental level to be tested. If the examiner allowed the talkative child to converse at will and answered all questions not pertinent to the solving of the problem, the child would be in no way handicapped by an unfamiliar situation, and the silent child would be left free from irritating interference.

*Purposeful effort.*— How could whole-hearted effort be secured without verbal urging? As has been pointed out in Chapter I, the very absence of verbal direction leads to better effort on the part of many children. The reduction in the number of pieces of equipment is also an aid to increasing interest, especially in the distractible child.

In order to free the subject from emotional disturbance so far as possible it was decided to allow the presence of an older companion whenever this was desired, and for the same reason a small display board that could be used almost anywhere was substituted for the large table (see the frontispiece).

A rapid changing of blocks, a complete change of objects after using two or three blocks, a technique of first hiding the face of the block from the child and then suddenly revealing it would all present a challenge to his attention that would almost certainly inspire an attempt at a correct response. A convenient arrangement of materials in trays would so free the examiner from administrative details that her own enthusiasm could be communicated to the child.

*Number of trials.*— How many trials should the child be allowed with each stimulus block? If he were allowed as many trials as he needed for success, practice with one might influence response to another, and the final result might be due more largely to repeated trial and error than to ability. On the other hand, a restriction to one trial on each block would largely prevent testing the ability "to make adjustments to secure a desired end." (See Symonds, 34, for a discussion of this question.) As a compromise it was decided that not more than three trials would be allowed, that the child would not be urged to make even three trials if he were satisfied with fewer, and that the amount of credit to be given to each trial would be decided later.

*Objective record.*— Since each object could be placed in the stimulus block in many different positions and since the child changes from one response to another very rapidly, how could the examiner secure an objective record of all these varied responses and still be free to give the greater part of her attention to maintaining rapport with the child?

Each of the clearly distinguishable positions for each object was recorded on the scoring sheet by an appropriate diagram. (See Plate II for a sample section of this sheet.) These ranged from one position for the ball to six positions each for the cups, the tops, the boxes, and the shaker. The diagrams were so arranged on the scoring sheet that the correct response for Form A was always found at the extreme left and that for Form B at the extreme right. All the other positions for one object were grouped together, and separate series were clearly marked off from each other.

The scoring sheet was clipped to a light board, and the record was made with a short pencil carried between the first and second fingers. Marking the order of responses by the simple figures 1, 2, 3, under the appropriate diagram could thus be done with a minimum of attention from the examiner and the subject.

PLATE II

SECTION OF THE FIRST SCORING SHEET WITH SYMBOLS

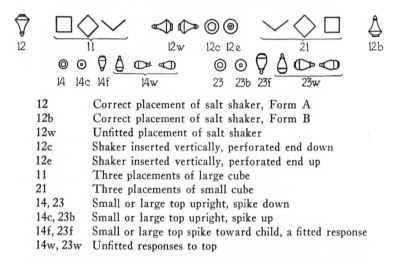

| 12 | Correct placement of salt shaker, Form A |
| 12b | Correct placement of salt shaker, Form B |
| 12w | Unfitted placement of salt shaker |
| 12c | Shaker inserted vertically, perforated end down |
| 12e | Shaker inserted vertically, perforated end up |
| 11 | Three placements of large cube |
| 21 | Three placements of small cube |
| 14, 23 | Small or large top upright, spike down |
| 14c, 23b | Small or large top upright, spike up |
| 14f, 23f | Small or large top spike toward child, a fitted response |
| 14w, 23w | Unfitted responses to top |

*Time score.*— Should a careful time score be kept? Preliminary work with the material had shown great variations in the total time required. This had seemed to be a function of personality rather than of intelligence. Thorndike has pointed out that "time for making mistakes is of little significance" (36, p. 482). To time accurately each correct response separately from the incorrect and from the time necessary for presenting and removing the material would require all the attention of one examiner. It was therefore decided to allow each child as much time as he desired and to keep a record merely of the number of whole minutes required.

## Problems Incurred in the Selection of Subjects

*Representative sampling.*— What should be the criteria for securing a representative sampling of the population? Since it was obviously impossible to secure an actual random sampling of all children of preschool age, the more carefully the selection was made the more closely would the sample obtained approximate the ideal random sampling. The principles of selection employed for this study were: (1) equal numbers of each sex and (2) a percentage of cases in each social category equal to the percentage of that category in the Minneapolis population, according to the census of 1920.[4] All cases of very evident negativism were thrown out, but those where negativism was merely suspected as affecting the results were included in the data. This procedure is in accordance with what must be done when actually seeking to measure an individual child's intelligence. Since a test that would be useful in measuring all races was needed, no attempt was made to confine the subjects exclusively to "North Europeans," "American-born," or "whites." On the contrary, a special effort was made to include a few South Europeans, Hebrews, negroes, and Asiatics. The distribution of cases actually used in the standardization of the test is given in Table IV, which shows how closely the group for each year conformed to the socio-economic distribution in the population.

*Delimitation of age group.*— How should the age groups be defined? Two-, three-, four-, and five-year-olds were selected as the age groups to which this material might appeal. Each group took its name from its mean age, and the age range was from one year and six months to two years, five months, and thirty days.

[4] A better basis of selection than that of the percentage of men in each social category might have been the percentage of children whose fathers are in each category, since the extreme numerical difference in size of family between groups I and II and groups V and VI may materially disturb the ratio. There are, however, no census data that would make such a selection possible.

## TABLE IV

### Distribution of Cases in Percentages by Age and by Social Category

| Group | Social Category | | | | | |
|---|---|---|---|---|---|---|
| | I | II | III | IV | V | VI |
| Total population | 5.4 | 6.3 | 37.3 | 24.3 | 14.9 | 11.8 |
| Two-year-olds | 6.0 | 6.0 | 36.0 | 24.0 | 16.0 | 12.0 |
| Three-year-olds | 6.0 | 6.0 | 36.0 | 24.0 | 16.0 | 12.0 |
| Four-year-olds | 4.0 | 8.0 | 36.0 | 24.0 | 16.0 | 12.0 |
| Five-year-olds | 6.0 | 6.0 | 36.0 | 24.0 | 16.0 | 12.0 |
| All ages | 5.5 | 6.5 | 36.0 | 24.0 | 16.0 | 12.0 |

*Number of cases per group.*— How many children should be obtained for each representative age group and how many of these should be given retests? Which form of the test should be given first? There has been wide divergence in both practice and theory on this point. In the case of group or individual testing of older children it has been customary to secure records for as large a population as possible. But the greatly increased difficulty of locating a large number of preschool children is reflected in the fact that norms have frequently been based upon a very few cases. Bronner implies that any test element that has been applied to any 50 children is "adequately standardized" (4, pp. 11–12). A more trustworthy procedure would seem to be that of occasionally taking stock and judging by the standard error of the difference of the means whether enough cases have been tested to insure stable norms.

For this study the decision was to collect the cases in representative subgroups of 25 children each and then by combining these subgroups to determine whether or not more cases were necessary.

*Interval between tests.*—What time interval should elapse between a test with one form and a retest with the other? The rapid acceleration of the growth curve in children at these early ages indicates that the interval between tests that are to be compared for reliability should be short. It was therefore determined that no retest would be given later than one week after the first test.

*Source of supply.*— How could one person find opportunity to test individually a sufficient number of preschool children without a prohibitive expenditure of time and effort? It was made possible by the fact that (1) the time required for one test was short; (2) that only a small amount of information was required about each child, (3) and that the test could be administered with facility in any place, so that it was possible to obtain cases from almost every social agency, as well as from various types of private homes. The distribution of cases according to the four sources of supply is shown in Table V.

TABLE V

DISTRIBUTION OF CASES BY AGE AND BY SOURCE OF SUPPLY

| SOURCE OF SUPPLY | AGE GROUP IN YEARS | | | | TOTAL |
| --- | --- | --- | --- | --- | --- |
| | 2 | 3 | 4 | 5 | |
| Members of nursery school or children brought to the Institute of Child Welfare by their parents.................. | 24 | 28 | 21 | 13 | 86 |
| Children brought to the public schools by older members of the family...... | 12 | 20 | 2 | 1 | 35 |
| Children visited in their homes............. | 5 | 7 | 1 | 0 | 13 |
| Children secured at public welfare agencies or brought to the institute by workers in such agencies........... | 59 | 45 | 76 | 86 | 266 |
| Total...................................... | 100 | 100 | 100 | 100 | 400 |

SUMMARY

1. The Object-Fitting Test originated in (a) the need for a nonlanguage test for young children in southeastern Asia, (b) the need for a nonlanguage test for the preschool deaf, and (c) a study of perception in young children.

2. Decisions reached in the preliminary construction of material were (a) to use part of the perception material for the construction of a nonlanguage test; (b) to make two forms as equally matched as possible; (c) to make the test as short as possible and still retain its original validity and reliability; (d) to standardize twenty blocks that seemed highly discriminative, small in size, and unequivocal in scoring; (e) to provide a fore-exercise in which to establish "mind-set"; (f) to allow conversation not pertinent to the test; (g) to avoid all verbal direction; (h) to allow the presence of an older companion; (i) to eliminate all unnecessary administrative detail so that the examiner might be free to retain the child's attention more effectively; (j) to allow each child to make from one to three responses to each block according to his own desire and to determine the credit for these responses on the basis of the results secured; and (k) to record time to the nearest whole minute with no restriction as to time allowed.

3. Decisions reached as to the selection of subjects were (a) to use equal numbers of each sex; (b) to keep the percentage of cases from each social category equal to the percentage of that category in the Minneapolis population according to the census of 1920; (c) to throw out only those cases where negativism was unmistakable; (d) to define the groups for each year by the mean; (e) to collect all cases in representative subgroups of 25 children each and to combine groups until a stable mean was obtained; (f) to give no retest later than one week after the first test; and (g) to secure cases through the Institute of Child Welfare, through social agencies, and through private homes.

# CHAPTER III

# THE STANDARDIZATION OF THE TEST

## PRELIMINARY CONSIDERATIONS

*Criteria of reliability and validity.* — Other things being equal, the method of scoring that gives the most consistent results with the largest number of cases should be chosen. This self-consistency can be measured either by the comparative number of positive and negative changes in response from test to test or by a coefficient of correlation between scores on the two test forms.

The validity of new tests for older children is commonly checked by comparison with school marks, teacher-ratings, school grade, or some Binet test. Such criteria are not available in work with the preschool child. This forces the investigator to rely upon the criterion of chronological age. Judged by this criterion that method of scoring should be chosen that shows the highest percentage of increase in number of successful performances with increase in chronological age.

This discriminative capacity may be measured by four methods, i.e., (1) by a comparison of the means for the various years, (2) by the discriminative value of the test as shown by Woodrow's formula:

$$DV = \frac{\text{Av.}_2 - \text{Av.}_1}{\frac{1}{2}(\sigma_1 + \sigma_2)},$$

(3) by the ratio between the difference of two year means and the standard error of this difference, (4) by the same ratio for two groups of equal chronological age but known or suspected to be of differing mental ability, such as children from homes of the lowest and the highest economic status.

*Time scores.* — The reasons for not determining performance time in seconds or split seconds have been given (Chapter II, page 34). For comparative purposes, however, certain data on the total time taken for the Object-Fitting Test have been given.

The two-year time range was from 5 to 19 minutes and the five-year from 5 to 10 minutes. The self-reliability coefficient of the time scores for the two-year-olds was but $.242\pm.19$; for the five-year-olds, $.324\pm.18$. The difference between the mean times of performance for these widely separated age groups is 3.7 minutes, which is but 1.37 times the standard error.[1] These figures are of no statistical significance but indicate another reason why time was not included as a factor in determining scores.

*Response to be credited.* — The difference of opinion and practice as to which response should receive credit when more than one trial has been given is illustrated in the data of Table II. For fourteen blocks in the Object-Fitting Test a comparison was made of the number of changes in response from test to retest when the last response was credited instead of the first response. Only those responses were counted in which (1) the change was from incorrect to correct (positive change) or from correct to incorrect (negative change), and (2) those in which the change in method (i. e., from crediting the first response to crediting the last response) would cause a change in the credit given. If by both methods there was the same response to the two tests or the same type of change, no change was counted.

By the method of first response there were 58 positive and 25 negative changes, a total of 83 changes in 200 cases. By the method of crediting only the last response there were but 25 positive and 22 negative changes, a total of 47. It would seem, therefore, that crediting only the last response blots out certain practice effects that would otherwise be shown by positive changes in score but that crediting on this

[1] The examinations were timed to the nearest whole minute from the time the first block was put before the child until his placing or refusing to place the last object. Naturally the writer does not imagine that she has measured any intricate psychological reaction time by this simple procedure. She merely wanted to obtain a general idea of the average or approximate time of the test, since this is a factor that has been used heretofore for scoring performance tests.

basis has little effect on the number of negative changes. It was decided to base scores upon the last response.

*Symbols for responses.* — Since there were nearly one hundred different types of response recorded separately, it was necessary to adopt some system of symbolization in order to facilitate work with the data. The symbols for series IV, together with a diagrammatic representation of the position of each object thus designated, have been shown in Plate II (page 33). It was impractical to include here the meaning of each of the other symbols.

## RAW DATA ON LAST RESPONSES

*The subjects.* — In all, 266 girls and 291 boys were tested, a total of 557. Series of representative samplings were built up for the determination of norms. The distribution of these cases has been shown in Table IV. There were 50 children in each year to whom Form A was given first and 50 children to whom Form B was given first. These 100 children in each year were divided into four groups of 25 subjects, each group constituting a representative sampling.[2] The method of building up the larger groups by various combinations of subgroups is illustrated in Table VI, giving the distribution for the two-year-olds. The Aa

TABLE VI

METHOD OF BUILDING UP A REPRESENTATIVE YEAR GROUP FROM
REPRESENTATIVE SUBGROUPS

| Group | OCCUPATIONAL CATEGORY | | | | | | TOTAL |
|---|---|---|---|---|---|---|---|
| | I | II | III | IV | V | VI | |
| Aa | 2 | 1 | 9 | 6 | 4 | 3 | 25 |
| Ba | 1 | 2 | 9 | 6 | 4 | 3 | 25 |
| AaBb | 2 | 1 | 9 | 6 | 4 | 3 | 25 |
| BaAb | 1 | 2 | 9 | 6 | 4 | 3 | 25 |
| Total | 6 | 6 | 36 | 24 | 16 | 12 | 100 |

[2] As will be shown in Table XVII, the number of cases was in every instance sufficient to establish a stable mean.

group were tested once with Form A, the Ba group once with Form B, the AaBb group with Form A first and with Form B second, and the BaAb group with Form B first and Form A second. Since each subgroup had a socio-economic distribution similar to that of the others, it was possible to draw conclusions from the data that might otherwise have been highly fallacious.

*Age groups.*—The mean chronological age of each year group was in every case within six days of the age for which the group was named. For the two-year-olds the mean age was one year, eleven months, and twenty-nine days; for the three-year-olds, exactly three years; for the four-year-olds, four years and six days; and for the five-year-olds, four years, eleven months, and twenty-seven days.

*Retests to determine reliability.*—In each year one subgroup (AaBb) of 25 children was given Form A first and retested with Form B within a week; another (BaAb) was given Form B first, followed by Form A. The mean number of days between tests is shown in Table VII.

TABLE VII

MEAN NUMBER OF DAYS BETWEEN TESTING

| GROUP | YEAR | | | |
|---|---|---|---|---|
| | 2 | 3 | 4 | 5 |
| AaBb | 3.5 | 3.7 | 3.0 | 3.3 |
| BaAb | 1.8 | 2.8 | 2.8 | 2.8 |

SOME UNSATISFACTORY SCORING METHODS

*The year-scale method.*—The method used by Kohs (18) in his Block Design Test was used for determining the year-scale location of each stimulus block in the O-F Test. The percentage of successes out of four hundred responses to each block in Form A is shown in Table VIII and is graphically portrayed in Plate III. The rise of all the curves is surprisingly regular as compared with the result of Kohs, and in no case is there an appreciable drop in the curve of an upper age below that of a lower age.[3] Blocks 1, 2, 3, 7, and 14 are not highly discriminative between the fourth and fifth years; blocks 1, 7, 13, and 15, between the ages of three and four; or blocks 6, 8, 9, 10, 13, and 15, between the second and third years. Blocks 1, 7, 8, 13, and

## TABLE VIII

PERCENTAGE OF CORRECT RESPONSES TO EACH BLOCK IN FORM A AMONG CHILDREN OF THE FOUR AGE LEVELS

| BLOCK | YEAR | | | | TOTAL |
|-------|------|------|------|------|-------|
|       | 2    | 3    | 4    | 5    |       |
| 1     | 91   | 100  | 100  | 100  | 98    |
| 2     | 29   | 71   | 100  | 99   | 75    |
| 3     | 11   | 66   | 97   | 97   | 68    |
| 4     | 4    | 21   | 56   | 81   | 41    |
| 5     | 4    | 34   | 75   | 94   | 52    |
| 6     | 8    | 24   | 58   | 86   | 37    |
| 7     | 58   | 96   | 98   | 100  | 88    |
| 8     | 4    | 10   | 36   | 49   | 25    |
| 9     | 0    | 0    | 19   | 51   | 18    |
| 10    | 0    | 2    | 27   | 68   | 26    |
| 11    | 8    | 34   | 76   | 94   | 55    |
| 12    | 4    | 29   | 69   | 91   | 49    |
| 13    | 0    | 5    | 10   | 24   | 4     |
| 14    | 4    | 24   | 50   | 56   | 34    |
| 15    | 1    | 4    | 11   | 44   | 15    |

15 fail to cross the 50 per cent line and seem to be, on the whole, least discriminative, but the positions of the first two entirely above the median line of success and of the other three entirely below it indicate that each does contribute something of its own to the total picture.

If each block were located at the point where its curve crosses the line of 50 per cent success, the relative positions of each would be approximately as shown in Plate III. Success with the various blocks would then receive mental-age

[3] In Plate VIII there is a diagrammatic representation of each block and of the objects accompanying it, and a complete description of all the material is given in Part II.

PLATE III

Y<small>EAR</small>-S<small>CALE</small> D<small>ATA</small>

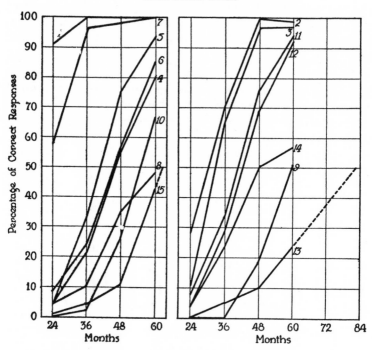

credit as shown in Table IX. But since this is at best a crude method of scoring it did not seem worth while to work out scores on this basis.

*The "total rights" point-score method.* — By this method one point was given for each correct response to a stimulus block, the total possible score being fifteen. The distribution of scores for the hundred AaBb and BaAb tests at each age level is shown in Table X. There is a fairly good spread of scores at each age and a very evident increase of score with increase in chronological age. The self-reliability seems surprisingly high for a performance test until one remembers the large part that chance and time factors have formerly been allowed to play in the scoring of such tests.

TABLE IX

MENTAL-AGE CREDIT IN MONTHS FOR INDIVIDUAL BLOCKS

| BLOCK | MA | BLOCK | MA |
|-------|-----|-------|-----|
| 2 | 18 | 9 | 59 |
| 3 | 21 | 10 | 55 |
| 4 | 46 | 11 | 40 |
| 5 | 41 | 12 | 42 |
| 6 | 44 | 13 | 82 |
| 7 | 21 | 14 | 48 |
| 8 | 61 | 15 | 62 |

In assembling the two forms of the test, pairs of blocks and different presentations of the same block had been matched on the basis of approximately equal difficulty. During the process of collecting data certain ones of these soon appeared to be less reliable and more subject to chance response than others. Nevertheless, all subjects were given the complete test as first planned. Then a check-up of the curves of the increasing percentage of correct responses from year to year showed several wide divergences between the four sampling groups. There was, on the whole, a striking similarity in the form of the curves for a particular block, as well as a distinct and fairly regular increase in percentage of success with increase in chronological age. But the curves of the two most doubtful pairs, A7–B6 and A14–B14, were widely divergent. On block A7–B6 presented to the two-year-olds group Aa had 76 per cent success, and group Ba only 28 per cent, a difference of 48 points; at three years, group Ab had 100 per cent success, and group Ba only 60 per cent, a difference of 40 points; at four years, group Ab had 100 per cent success, and group Bb had only 80 per cent, a difference of 20 points; at five years group

TABLE X

DISTRIBUTION OF "TOTAL RIGHTS" SCORES AMONG CHILDREN OF THE
FOUR AGE LEVELS

| SCORE POINT | YEAR | | | |
|---|---|---|---|---|
| | 2 | 3 | 4 | 5 |
| 15 | .... | .... | .... | 6 |
| 14 | .... | .... | 1 | 11 |
| 13 | .... | .... | 4 | 13 |
| 12 | .... | 2 | 5 | 18 |
| 11 | 1* | 4 | 15 | 16 |
| 10 | 1* | 2 | 15 | 9 |
| 9 | .... | 5 | 13 | 13 |
| 8 | .... | 12 | 11 | 7 |
| 7 | 1 | 12 | 10 | 3 |
| 6 | 1 | 19 | 9 | 2 |
| 5 | 2 | .... | 8 | 2 |
| 4 | 9 | 9 | 7 | .... |
| 3 | 9 | 18 | 2 | .... |
| 2 | 37 | 11 | .... | .... |
| 1 | 31 | 6 | .... | .... |
| 0 | 8 | .... | .... | .... |
| Total | 100 | 100 | 100 | 100 |
| Mean Aa | 2.760 | 4.920 | 8.000 | 10.840 |
| $SD$ of Mean | .406 | .406 | .560 | .370 |
| $SD$ | 2.290 | 2.310 | 2.830 | 1.890 |
| $SD$ of $SD$ | .330 | .330 | .400 | .290 |
| Pearson $r$: | | | | |
| AaBb | .76 | .90 | .95 | .81 |
| BaAb | .42 | .84 | .82 | .91 |

* Both of these extreme cases occur in the AaBb group and explain the
difference in reliability coefficient between AaBb and BaAb. They themselves have thus far baffled explanation. The bimodality in the third year
appears in both groups and may be due to the fact that blocks 2, 3, and
7 are widely separated in difficulty from the other blocks. As will be
shown later, blocks A14 and B14 proved to be very unreliable and subject to chance failures in the fifth year. This may be the cause for the
drop at score 10.

Ab had 100 per cent success, and group Bb only 88 per cent, a difference of 12 points. Thus for this block there is a total of 120 points divergence, in terms of percentage, between the lowest and highest groups. Table XI shows data for each block. Blocks A14–B14, and A7–B6 are shown to be very unreliable from group to group, and blocks A6–B7, A11–B11, A12–B12, although more reliable, are far from being as consistent as the others.

TABLE XI

DIFFERENCE IN PERCENTAGE OF SUCCESS ON FORM A BETWEEN THE
LOWEST AND THE HIGHEST TEST GROUP

| BLOCK | NUMBER OF POINTS OF DIVERGENCE * | BLOCK | NUMBER OF POINTS OF DIVERGENCE |
|---|---|---|---|
| 1 | 4 | 9 | 44 |
| 3 | 60 | 10 | 36 |
| 4 | 56 | 11 | 92 |
| 5 | 60 | 12 | 84 |
| 6 | 96 | 13 | 28 |
| 7 | 120 | 14 | 148 |
| 8 | 48 | 15 | 64 |

* Since the percentages were based upon equal numbers of cases, it was possible to add them to find a measure of the divergence between curves.

The self-reliability of each pair of blocks was then checked by comparing the two responses made to it by each of the 200 children who had retests. These data are given in Table XII, which should be read as follows: On block A1–B1, 97 per cent of the subjects who made a correct response to one form followed it by a correct response to the other, while on block A14–B14 only 21 per cent did so. On block A1–B1 only 1.5 per cent of all subjects made a correct response in the case of one form and a no-choice response in the other, while on block A6–B7, 4 per cent and on block A7–B6, 5.5 per cent made this decided change in response. In view of these facts, blocks A6–B7, A7–B6, and A14–B14, which failed in two out of three checks, were discarded as being unreliable. Blocks 6 and 7 were evidently too different to be matched, and in the case of block 14 there were too many round objects that would approximately fit the block.

TABLE XII

PERCENTAGE OF CHANGE BETWEEN TESTS

| BLOCK | PERCENTAGE CORRECT ON ONE WHO WERE CORRECT ON BOTH | PERCENTAGE WHO MADE CORRECT RESPONSE IN THE CASE OF ONE FORM AND NO-CHOICE RESPONSE IN THE OTHER |
|---|---|---|
| 1 | 97 | 1.5 |
| 2 | 89 | 1.0 |
| 3 | 85 | 2.5 |
| 4 | 78 | 1.0 |
| 5 | 82 | 1.5 |
| 6 | 55 | 4.0 |
| 7 | 71 | 5.5 |
| 8 | 48 | 0.0 |
| 9 | 56 | 0.0 |
| 10 | 64 | 0.0 |
| 11 | 69 | 0.5 |
| 12 | 73 | 0.5 |
| 13 | 44 | 0.0 |
| 14 | 21 | 1.0 |
| 15 | 30 | 0.0 |

"Total rights" scores on the remaining twelve pairs of blocks would doubtless show increased reliability and a sharper increase of success with increasing maturity, but since a range of scores from 0 to 12 is hardly enough for fine discrimination through four years, no such scores were computed.

"*Weighted*" *scoring methods.*—In spite of much theoretical discussion as to the weighting of scores, it was not thought worth while to try out any weighted scoring of these blocks. The accumulated experimental evidence against such procedures has been well summed up by Anderson (1).

## Point-Score Method with Partial Credit for Partial Success

*Derivation of method.* — The validity of this method is shown by sharply increasing percentages of success. While the writer was testing the children, it became quite evident that many of those who were unable to select and fit in the correct object for any given block nevertheless had the ability to make some adjustments to the new situation. Some turned the object chosen until its long axis paralleled that of the recess; others chose an object whose outline in cross section was similar in form to that of the recess, matching circular with circular, rectangular with rectangular, or irregular with irregular. Still others seemed to make choices purely on the basis of size; while with the cup blocks, any cup, regardless of perfect fit, was increasingly satisfactory with the increasing maturity of the subjects. Since any adaptation of this kind partially meets the accepted criteria of intelligence, a carefully detailed analysis of all such responses was undertaken. A tabulation was made of the number of subjects in each subgroup making each particular response at each age level. Comparisons of these showed that certain of these error responses were as reliable from subgroup to subgroup and increased in percentage of occurrence as regularly as the correct responses.

Table XIII gives the percentage of children making each

## TABLE XIII

Percentage Making Error Responses to Blocks A12–B12

| Year Group | Type of Error Response in Percentages | | | | | | | | | Total |
|---|---|---|---|---|---|---|---|---|---|---|
| | 14, 23 | 21 | 14W, 23W | 14F, 23F | 14c, 23b | 12W | 12e, 12c | 11 | X | |
| 2 | 7 | 15 | 1 | 3 | 20 | 0 | 13 | 2 | 40 | 101 |
| 3 | 7 | 13 | 8 | 17 | 20 | 4 | 25 | 0 | 6 | 100 |
| 4 | 0 | 10 | 10 | 45 | 10 | 6 | 19 | 0 | 0 | 100 |
| 5 | 22 | 0 | 0 | 56 | 11 | 0 | 11 | 0 | 0 | 100 |
| All ages | 7 | 12 | 4 | 16 | 18 | 2 | 18 | 1 | 22 | 100 |

type of error response to block 12. It must be interpreted by the symbols in Plate II, page 34, and it should be read as follows: Of the two-year-olds making incorrect responses to block 12, 7 per cent inserted a top point down, 15 per cent inserted the small cube, and so on. Note how the percentages for the majority of error responses decrease with increasing chronological age or vary greatly from year to year, while the responses 14F, 23F (placing a top upon its side with the vertex at the narrow end of the shaker recess —a *fitted* response) steadily increase in frequency of occurrence.

### TABLE XIV

#### PAIRED RESPONSES TO BLOCKS A4–B4

| | CORRECT (C) | ADJUSTED (F) | | | | UNADJUSTED (W) | | | | | No CHOICE (X) | TOTAL FOR EACH TYPE OF PAIRING* |
| | | 3F | 4F | 6F | 5F | 5c, 6c | 3c | 4W | 5W, 6W | 3W | | |
|---|---|---|---|---|---|---|---|---|---|---|---|---|
| C | **71** | 11 | 4 | 0 | 1 | 2 | 0 | 0 | 0 | 0 | 2 | |
| 3F | | **35** | 6 | 2 | 1 | 4 | 3 | 1 | 0 | 1 | 1 | 2 |
| 4F | | | **6** | 0 | 2 | 0 | 1 | 0 | 0 | 0 | 7 | 1 |
| 6F | | | | **0** | 0 | 0 | 0 | 0 | 0 | 0 | 0 | 8 |
| 5F | | | | | **0** | 0 | 0 | 0 | 0 | 0 | 1 | 0 |
| 5c, 6c | | | | | | **5** | 3 | 1 | 2 | 0 | 4 | 2 |
| 3c | | | | | | | **0** | 0 | 0 | 0 | 4 | 9 |
| 4W | | | | | | | | **2** | 0 | 1 | 2 | 10 |
| 5W, 6W | | | | | | | | | **0** | 1 | 0 | 5 |
| 3W | | | | | | | | | | **0** | 0 | 10 |
| X | | | | | | | | | | | **13** | 21 |
| Total | | | | | | | | | | | | **132** |

\* Read diagonally, then horizontally.

Reliability and validity are shown by the pairing of responses. The self-reliability of each error response was determined for block A4–B4 (see Table XIV). For this purpose the exact response of each of the 200 children to each block in Form A was compared with his response to the corresponding block in Form B. This table is to be read as follows: 71 subjects responded correctly to both presentations of this block; 35 tried both times to adjust the pencil (3) by turning it so that it "fitted" in the right direction (3F); 6 tried both times to adjust the box (4) on its large side by turning it so that it "fitted" in the right direction (4F); no subject tried both times to adjust either the bowl (6) or the spool (5F). Eleven subjects responded correctly to one presentation and with 3F to the other; 4 re-

TABLE XV

SUMMARY OF PAIRED RESPONSES TO BLOCKS A4–B4

|  | C | F | W | X | TOTAL FOR EACH TYPE OF PAIRING * | AMOUNT OF CHANGE |
|---|---|---|---|---|---|---|
| C | 71 | 16 | 2 | 2 |  |  |
| F |  | 52 | 10 | 9 | 2 | Extreme |
| W |  |  | 15 | 10 | 11 | Moderate |
| X |  |  |  | 13 | 36 | Slight |
| Total |  |  |  |  | 151 | None |

* Read diagonally, then horizontally.

sponded correctly to one presentation and with 4F to the other. No subject responded correctly to one presentation and with 3c (pencil on end) to the other; no subject responded correctly to one presentation and with 4W (box not adjusted as to direction) to the other. Two subjects responded correctly to one presentation and made no object-fitting response to the other.

From this it is evident that the error responses 3F and 4F are the only ones paired more frequently with a correct response or with themselves than with other incorrect responses. They are therefore the only error responses to A4–B4 that should receive credit. In Table XV the diagonal column of figures running from upper left to lower right distinguishes the pairs showing no change in response from those showing progressively greater change. In Table XVI note how consistently each type of response is paired with itself or with a similar type.

## TABLE XVI

DEGREE OF CHANGE IN PAIRED RESPONSES TO INDIVIDUAL BLOCKS

| BLOCK | NO CHANGE | SLIGHT CHANGE | MODERATE CHANGE | EXTREME CHANGE |
|-------|-----------|---------------|-----------------|----------------|
| 1 | 197 | 1 | 0 | 2 |
| 2 | 178 | 20 | 0 | 2 |
| 3 | 160 | 27 | 8 | 5 |
| 5 | 150 | 35 | 14 | 1 |
| 8 | 122 | 65 | 13 | 0 |
| 9 | 125 | 69 | 6 | 0 |
| 10 | 133 | 55 | 12 | 0 |
| 11 | 127 | 57 | 15 | 1 |
| 12 | 139 | 53 | 7 | 1 |
| 13 | 122 | 67 | 11 | 0 |
| 15 | 151 | 47 | 2 | 0 |

Credits were assigned on the following basis. Other things being equal, the error response that should receive most credit is one that (1) increases in percentage of total errors most sharply and regularly with increase in maturity, and (2) is paired most often with correct or "fitted" responses and least often with no-choice or "unadjusted" responses.

A careful comparison of all the data with these criteria in mind resulted in the list of arbitrary credits allowed to various responses given below.

CREDIT ALLOWED FOR EACH TYPE OF RESPONSE TO BLOCKS 1–5 AND 8–13 [4]

11 points for each of the following types of response:

1. A totally correct placement in any block.
2. In block A9–B10 (the rounded cup) (a) placing *either* cup in correct position but with handle not pushed down; (b) placing *correct* cup on its side in the recess even though the top and bottom are reversed in position.
3. In block A10–B9 (the flaring cup) (a) placing *either* cup in correct position but with handle not pushed down; (b) placing *correct* cup on its side in Form A and *incorrect* cup on its side

[4] Compare with the revised scoring sheet shown in Plate IX at the end of this volume.

in Form B even though the top and bottom are reversed in position.

6 points for the following:

1. In block 2 (box), placing the ball (1). (This affects only the second and third years but is very significant there.)

4 points for each of the following:

1. In block 4 (box on edge) placing the pencil so that it "fits" in the right direction (3F).

2. In block 8 (square block on edge) placing the long block so that it "fits" in the *direction* of its long axis whether laid horizontally over the recess or diagonally with one end in the recess (22F).

3. In block 12 (shaker) (a) placing shaker on its side even though top and bottom are reversed in position (12W); (b) placing either large or small top on its side with apex to small end of shaker recess (14F, 23F).

4. In block 13 (small cube on edge) placing small cube in an upright position (21).

3 points for the following:

1. In block 5 (single spool on side) (a) placing either the pencil or the small box with its long axis parallel to the long axis of the spool recess (3F, 4F); or (b) fitting the end of the small box into either end of the spool recess (4F).

2 points for each of the following:

1. In block 4 (box on edge) (a) placing box on largest side with its long axis parallel to recess (4F); or (b) fitting end of box into recess (4F).

2. In block 5 (single spool on side) placing spool in a vertical position in the recess (5c). (This seems to be analogous to the cup responses, where choice of correct object satisfied the child.)

1 point for each other incorrect response of an attempt to place an object in the recess, as opposed to no-choice responses, which received no credit.

CREDIT ALLOWED FOR EACH TYPE OF RESPONSE TO BLOCK 15

10 points for a correctly fitted response of 4 spools (C).

8 points for a correctly graded response of 4 spools (G).

6 points for (a) a response of 3 spools correctly graded in series (A); or (b) 7 or 8 trials, more than half of which are of spools laid on side (A).

4 points for ungraded responses of 3 to 6 trials at least half of which are of spools laid on side (W).

## TABLE XVII

RATIO OF THE DIFFERENCE OF THE MEANS TO THE STANDARD ERROR
OF DIFFERENCE

| GROUPS COMPARED | YEAR | | | |
|---|---|---|---|---|
| | 2 | 3 | 4 | 5 |
| 25Aa and 50Aa | 1.04 | .57 | .49 | .83 |
| 50Aa and 100a | 1.29 | .52 | .25 | 1.32 |
| 100a and 150a and b | 1.30 | .66 | .48 | 1.56 |
| 25Aa and 150a and b | .99 | .86 | .20 | 1.44 |

## TABLE XVIII

DISTRIBUTION OF OBJECT-FITTING SCORES AMONG CHILDREN OF THE
FOUR AGE LEVELS

| SCORE | YEAR | | | |
|---|---|---|---|---|
| | 2 | 3 | 4 | 5 |
| 130–139 | .... | .... | 3 | 12 |
| 120–129 | .... | .... | 10 | 28 |
| 110–119 | .... | 3 | 15 | 36 |
| 100–109 | .... | 4 | 23 | 28 |
| 90–99 | 2 | 10 | 28 | 25 |
| 80–89 | 0 | 10 | 26 | 11 |
| 70–79 | 1 | 14 | 19 | 7 |
| 60–69 | 2 | 31 | 15 | 3 |
| 50–59 | 4 | 21 | 7 | .... |
| 40–49 | 12 | 14 | 4 | .... |
| 30–39 | 26 | 23 | .... | .... |
| 20–29 | 59 | 19 | .... | .... |
| 10–19 | 28 | 1 | .... | .... |
| 0–9 | 16 | .... | .... | .... |
| Total | 150 | 150 | 150 | 150 |
| Median | 25.4 | 58.6 | 91.4 | 110.3 |
| Percentage of lower age reaching or exceeding median of next higher | 4 | 8 | 13 | .... |

*Presentation of data on raw scores.* — 1. A stable mean.
The question propounded earlier in the present chapter as to whether 25 carefully selected cases were sufficient

PLATE IV

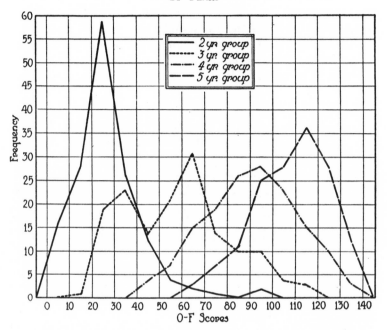

to establish a stable mean O-F score is answered by the data in Table XVII. This shows that the addition of 25, 50, and 150 additional cases to the original 25 in each year group caused no statistically significant change in the mean O-F score.

2. Distribution of scores. The distribution of six hundred O-F scores is shown in Table XVIII and in Plate IV. The percentile distribution is shown in Table XIX and in Plate V. Each decile curve shows a steady and definite increase from age to age. There is no drop in any curve from a higher to a lower age and no crossing of lines. The flattening out of the upper curves between the ages of four and five in the left-hand figures of Plate V indicates that the test is not adequate for the brighter children at these ages.

The same point is shown in the right-hand figure by the drawing together of curves for the fourth and fifth year.

No attempt was made to have a sampling at each month level that would be adequately representative of the various occupational groups in the population. When, therefore, the month-by-month increase in mean score was plotted, the result was a very different sort of curve from those shown in Plate V. The curve in Plate VI (page 59) reflects to a sur-

TABLE XIX

PERCENTILE DISTRIBUTION OF OBJECT-FITTING SCORES AMONG CHILDREN OF THE FOUR AGE LEVELS

| PERCENTILE | YEAR | | | |
|---|---|---|---|---|
| | 2 | 3 | 4 | 5 |
| Highest | 94 | 112 | 131 | 131 |
| 90 | 45 | 92 | 119 | 125 |
| 80 | 33 | 78 | 109 | 124 |
| 70 | 31 | 69 | 103 | 119 |
| 60 | 28 | 64 | 97 | 114 |
| 50 | 25 | 59 | 91 | 110 |
| 40 | 23 | 51 | 86 | 105 |
| 30 | 20 | 41 | 80 | 100 |
| 20 | 15 | 34 | 72 | 94 |
| 10 | 12 | 26 | 61 | 84 |
| Lowest | 00 | 14 | 45 | 66 |

prising degree the fluctuations in the proportion of groups I and II in the month sampling. Each low point marked X on the curve represents a month level in which no children in groups I or II chanced to be tested; each high point marked O represents a month level in which several children from groups I or II were tested but few or none from groups V and VI. The inference from Plates IV and V is that a representative sampling of 25 cases for each month level would show as regular an increase in O-F scores as do the representative year samplings.

3. Discriminative capacity. In each testing of a subgroup the difference between the mean scores for any two con-

# PLATE V

### Decile and Percentile Curves of Object-Fitting Scores Among Children of the Four Age Levels

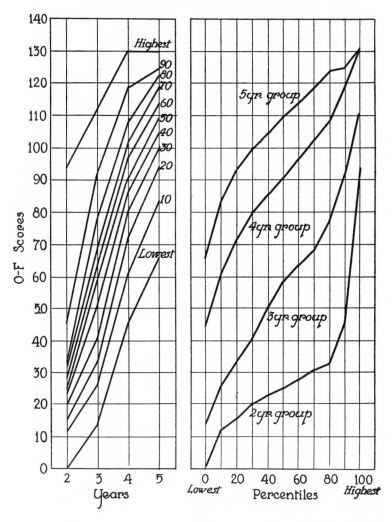

secutive years is statistically very significant, although the inadequacy of the test at the fifth year is again apparent (see Table XX). For those who prefer the discriminative value method of indicating comparisons the data as derived by Woodrow's formula are given in Table XXI.

4. Self-reliability. The self-reliability between Forms A and B as indicated by the Pearson correlation coefficient is shown in Table XXII. The lower coefficients when Form B

### TABLE XX

RATIO OF DIFFERENCE OF YEAR MEANS TO STANDARD DEVIATION OF DIFFERENCE

| Year Groups Compared | Ratio for 150 Tests in Each Year |
|---|---|
| 2 and 3 | 13.8 |
| 3 and 4 | 12.9 |
| 4 and 5 | 7.6 |

### TABLE XXI

DISCRIMINATIVE CAPACITY OF THE OBJECT-FITTING TEST AS SHOWN BY WOODROW'S FORMULA

| Year Groups Compared | $DV$ for 150 Tests in Each Year |
|---|---|
| 2 and 3 | 1.730 |
| 3 and 4 | 1.480 |
| 4 and 5 | 0.979 |

### TABLE XXII

SELF-RELIABILITY OF OBJECT-FITTING SCORES ON THE BASIS OF THE PEARSON CORRELATION COEFFICIENT

| Group | Year | | | |
|---|---|---|---|---|
| | 2 | 3 | 4 | 5 |
| 25 AaBb | .84 | .96 | .92 | .82 |
| 25 BaAb | .79 | .86 | .80 | .93 |

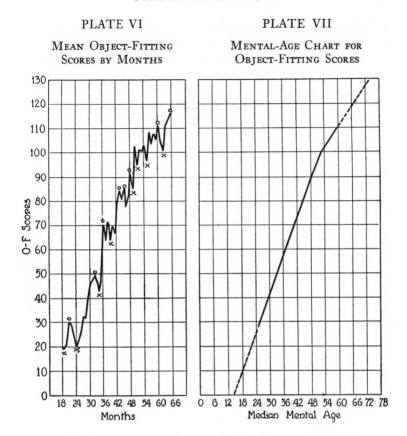

PLATE VI

MEAN OBJECT-FITTING
SCORES BY MONTHS

PLATE VII

MENTAL-AGE CHART FOR
OBJECT-FITTING SCORES

was given first seemed to be due to memory of the former presentation and were especially apparent in blocks 9, 10, and 11. For this reason Form A should be given first whenever possible.

5. Comparison of O-F scores with an outside criterion. The Minnesota Preschool Test was given to 125 children immediately after the O-F Test by the same examiner.[5] The distribution of these cases and the correlation between the two tests is shown in Table XXIII.

Although the nonlanguage O-F Test required from 4 to

[5] This test, which is soon to be published after several years of work to secure adequate standardization, is a verbal test similar to the Binet.

20 minutes to administer and the Minnesota Preschool Test from 20 to 50 minutes, the correlations for years three and four are as high as is frequently found for different applications of the same verbal test. In year two, the correlation of .52 indicates that the two tests are still measuring the same functions to a large extent but that certain factors gauged by one test are not gauged by the other. It appears probable that ability to use and understand spoken English is the most significant of these factors.

TABLE XXIII

DISTRIBUTION BY AGE AND OCCUPATIONAL CATEGORY IN OBJECT-FITTING AND MINNESOTA PRESCHOOL TEST *

| YEAR GROUP | CASES IN EACH OCCUPATIONAL CATEGORY | | | TOTAL TEST PAIRS | TOTAL INDIVIDUALS | PEARSON r |
|---|---|---|---|---|---|---|
| | I–II | III–IV | V–VI | | | |
| 2 years | 6 | 34 | 10 | 50 | 35 | .52 |
| 3 years | 6 | 30 | 14 | 50 | 33 | .85 |
| 4 years | 6 | 14 | 8 | 25 | 19 | .78 |
| Number required for a representative sampling of 50 cases | 6 | 30 | 14 | .... | .... | .... |

* Since the Object-Fitting Test does not adequately measure five-year-olds, no comparisons were made for this year level.

Negativistic and distractible children seemed to do better with the O-F Test, and the fact that the O-F Test was always given first operated to lower the O-F scores of shy children more than their scores on the Minnesota test. This effect was noted especially with certain of the younger children for whom the O-F material seemed to act as an icebreaker; they responded much more freely to the Minnesota test than at first seemed possible. The results of these factors tended to partially offset what was probably the most significant factor, the ability to use and to understand spoken English.

*Presentation of data on derived scores.* — 1. Derivation

of mental age scores and intelligence quotients. In view of the facts shown above in Plates V and VI it seemed best to reckon mental ages from the median scores of the representative year samples by means of the chart in Plate VII, page 59. The mental age for each O-F score is given in Table XXV, page 79. The mental ages below twenty-four months and above sixty months were merely estimated from projection of the line and are less reliable.

2. Comparison of mean intelligence quotients for occupational categories VI and I and II combined. Other investigations point toward an actual difference in the mean intelligence level of these groups. Table XXIV shows the results of a comparison of eighteen cases from I and II for

TABLE XXIV

COMPARISON OF MEAN *IQ* FOR GROUPS I AND II AND GROUP VI
THROUGH YEARS TWO, THREE, AND FOUR

| GROUP | NUMBER | MEAN *CA* | MEAN *IQ* | RATIO OF DIFFERENCE TO *SD* OF DIFFERENCE |
|---|---|---|---|---|
| I–II | 18 | 35.0 | 109.0 | 4.6 |
| VI | 18 | 35.5 | 93.7 | .... |

years two, three, and four (mean *CA*, 35 months) with the same number of cases from group VI (mean *CA*, 35.5). While the difference in mean *CA* is statistically very insignificant, the ratio of 4.6 between the difference in *IQ* and the standard error of this difference indicate that the Object-Fitting Test may be measuring a very real difference between the groups.[6]

[6] There are, however, certain selective factors at work that may tend to increase the apparent difference between groups I and II and group VI. Because of the character of the sources of supply, the extremes of each group are most likely to be included in the sampling. The more intelligent parents are most cooperative in bringing their children for testing, and the children of the least efficient parents in group VI are the ones commonly found in charge of social agencies.

## Summary

1. Endeavor was made to select the method of scoring that showed the highest reliability and validity.

2. The time score was found to be unreliable and non-discriminative of maturity.

3. The last response was found to be more reliable and less subject to the effect of practice than was the first response.

4. The year-scale method gave only a crude picture of the results.

5. The "total rights" point-score method was found to be both reliable and discriminative between year groups but lacked the finer calibration necessary for an individual test.

6. Certain blocks found to be less reliable and less discriminative were discarded.

7. "Weighted" scoring methods were rejected as not economical.

8. Certain "partial success" responses were proved to be as reliable and as discriminative as full success responses and were assigned partial credit.

9. The mean score on twenty-five tests was found to be not significantly different from the mean score on fifty, one hundred, or one hundred and fifty tests.

10. The month-by-month mean scores reflected the non-representative character of the month samplings, while the year means showed high discriminative capacity.

11. The Pearson coefficients of correlation between forms ranged from .79 to .96, with an average of .87.

12. The test correlated highly with a verbal scale given immediately following it.

13. An apparently significant difference was found between the mean intelligence quotients of groups of the highest and the lowest economic status.

## CHAPTER IV

## CONCLUSIONS AND A FORWARD LOOK

### Meeting the Criteria

To what extent does the Object-Fitting Test meet the criteria set forth in Chapter I?

1. *Intrinsic interest.* — It proves very interesting to practically every child exposed to it. Even those children with a strong negativistic tendency frequently show signs of glee when they find that an object will "just fit" and are drawn unconsciously into whole-hearted effort.

2. *Minimum of oral directions.* — It is given with no oral directions whatever.

3. *Briefness of attention span.* — Only a very few seconds of attention are required at one time, and the child solves or fails to solve the particular problem in that time. The great range in time scores is due to the variation in time between presentations of stimuli and serves to indicate how much a time score would have been determined by factors other than intelligence.

4. *Noncomplexity of material.* — The child is not confused by a multitude of pieces of material nor by being placed in an awkward position. Even the most difficult test series contains but six objects, all of which are well within the range of the child's experience.

5. *Equality of opportunity.* — This ideal can never be fully attained, but practically every child has had opportunity to see and to handle the objects used in this test, and no child has, previous to the test, met the exact stimulus-block situation presented to him. The use of the fore-exercise familiarizes all with the possibilities of the material, while the restriction to three trials for each block prevents undue practice effect.

6. *Noncommunicability.* — Even an adult would have some difficulty in giving a sufficiently accurate verbal description of the material so that another could carry out

directions as to the correct placing of each object. Certainly no young child can do so, and, in the absence of the material, an adult seeking to coach a child for the test might easily cause more wrong than right placements.

7. *Credit for actual responses.* — The point-score method was built up from actual results with the sample population. Each reliable and discriminative response, whether totally or partially correct, receives appropriate credit.

8. *Objective scoring.* — No two examiners familiar with the testing procedure can differ as to the interpretation of results.

9. *Adequate standardization.* — (a) Each subgroup contains a representative sampling of the Minneapolis population. (b) Each subgroup contains a sufficient number of cases to establish a stable mean. (c) The self-reliability between Forms A and B is high for each year group tested. (d) The test has high discriminative capacity, since it yields statistically significant differences between two groups known to differ in ability. (e) The test situation and response meet the commonly accepted definitions of general intelligence. (f) The test correlates highly with an outside criterion of intelligence at each age level, and the lower coefficient at year two indicates that the verbal test used as a criterion is measuring some factors not included in the nonlanguage Object-Fitting Test.

10. *Presentation of data.* — The description of subjects and the actual results of the standardization procedure are given in such detail that another experimenter should have no difficulty in repeating the procedures whenever desired.

## Meeting the Special Needs

To what extent does the Object-Fitting Test meet the special needs for a nonlanguage test?

1. *For the deaf.* — It gives the deaf child an equal chance with the normal child, since all directions are given in the language of gesture.

2. *For the non-English-speaking.* — The foreign-speaking child and the child with retarded speech development are

not handicapped by this test. Two Chinese children aged three and four who knew no English and were very timid nevertheless understood the problems and made scores entitling them to intelligence quotients of 130 and 129, respectively.

3. *For theoretical studies.* — This test should be of especial service in making comparisons of matched groups, since it (a) is applicable to all children; (b) requires a very brief time; (c) is portable; and (d) has been shown to require only twenty-five carefully selected cases per group.

## FUTURE USES FOR THE OBJECT-FITTING TEST AS A SCIENTIFIC INSTRUMENT

*Problems for which data are at hand.* — From the detailed record of responses now at hand the writer hopes at some future date to be enabled to make the following studies: (1) sex differences in response to the Object-Fitting Test; (2) perseverance in response as shown at different age levels and with specific objects; (3) persistence as a factor in success and its relation to chronological and mental age; (4) the effect of right-to-left position of objects upon first and last choices; (5) meaningful objects versus geometrical forms; (6) choice of objects as influenced by age and by occupational status; and (7) preference of young children for curved instead of angular objects.

*Other problems on which data can be easily secured.* — A few of the matched group comparisons having theoretical implications for which the Object-Fitting Test might appropriately be used are (1) a deaf group with a hearing group; (2) an English-speaking group with a non-English-speaking group; (3) one racial group with another racial group; (4) an institutional group with a home group of the same economic status; (5) an institutional group that has enjoyed a stimulating environment with an institutional group from the usual limiting environment; and (6) a group of children having two or more siblings immediately older with a group having two or more siblings immediately younger.

# PART II

MANUAL OF DIRECTIONS FOR THE ADMINIS-
TRATION OF THE OBJECT-FITTING TEST

# CHAPTER V

# MANUAL OF DIRECTIONS

## The Purpose of the Test

The Object-Fitting Test provides a means of classifying young children as to general intelligence by means of their nonverbal reactions to certain visual stimuli. These stimuli consist of a series of blocks containing recesses of various sizes and a group of common objects, certain ones of which may be fitted into the recesses. It is an intelligence test that can be given without the use of language on the part of either child or examiner. It is therefore especially adaptable for use with children who are deaf, who do not speak or understand the English language, or who have some language handicap. It may also be used for comparisons between such children and the normal English-speaking child.

## The Test Material

*The test proper.* — The material for the Object-Fitting Test consists of twenty-two small objects familiar to every child and fifteen papier-mâché blocks with depressions into which certain of these objects are to be fitted (see frontispiece and Plate VIII).

In Plate VIII the objects of each series are shown in the left-to-right order in which they are placed before the child for choice. The blocks are shown in the order in which they are presented to him, one by one. The objects are:[1]

FORE-EXERCISE: a celluloid swan, a small wooden top.
SERIES I: a gray rubber ball (1); a large, oblong box of nickel (2).
SERIES II: a large spool (5); a short pencil (3); a small aluminum bowl (6); a small, oblong box of nickel (4).

[1] The objects and blocks are numbered to correspond with the symbols used in the statistical treatment of the data.

# PLATE VIII

## Arrangement of Materials, Blocks, and Room Furniture for Test

### Materials of Object-Fitting Test

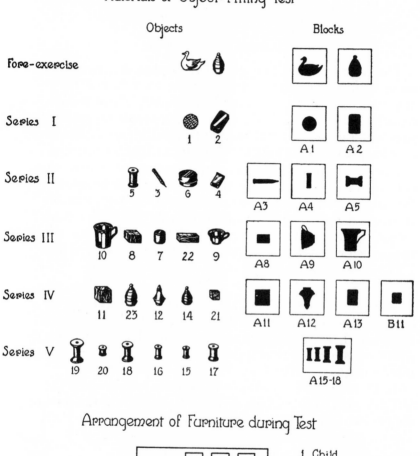

| | Objects | | Blocks |
|---|---|---|---|
| Fore-exercise | | | |
| Series I | 1  2 | | A1  A2 |
| Series II | 5  3  6  4 | | A3  A4  A5 |
| Series III | 10  8  7  22  9 | | A8  A9  A10 |
| Series IV | 11  23  12  14  21 | | A11  A12  A13  B11 |
| Series V | 19  20  18  16  15  17 | | A15-18 |

### Arrangement of Furniture during Test

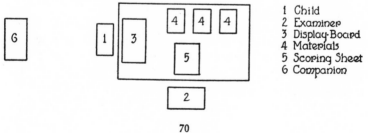

1 Child
2 Examiner
3 Display-Board
4 Materials
5 Scoring Sheet
6 Companion

SERIES III: an aluminum cup with flaring sides (10); a wooden block, 2 x 2 x 1 inches (8); a heavy black cylinder, 2½ x 1 inches (7); a wooden block, 1 x 1 x 3 inches (22); an aluminum cup with rounded sides (9).

SERIES IV: a wooden cube, 2 x 2 x 2 inches (11); a large wooden top (23); an aluminum salt shaker (12); a small wooden top (14); a wooden cube, 1 x 1 x 1 inches (21).

SERIES V: Six wooden spools of different sizes.

Fourteen of the blocks are 4 x 4 inches in size; the fifteenth block is 4 x 8 inches; their depth varies from ½ inch to 2 inches according to the object that each is designed to fit. These blocks were molded from paper pulp upon the objects themselves so as to secure a perfect fit and are painted a neutral gray with the recesses in solid black. The blocks for Form A are:

FORE-EXERCISE: swan laid on its side, small top laid on its side.

SERIES I: ball (A1); box on its largest side (A2).

SERIES II: pencil on its side (A3); box on its long edge (A4); large spool on its side (A5).

SERIES III: square block on its edge (A8); rounded cup on its side (A9); flaring cup on its side (A10).

SERIES IV: large cube on its side (A11); salt shaker on its side (A12); small cube on its edge (A13).

SERIES V: four graded spools laid side by side in order of their size (A15).

*Scoring material.* — The revised scoring sheets are shown in Plates IX and X; each drawing represents a possible response of the child. In the wide column at the extreme left are shown the objects, each series of toys arranged in the left-to-right order in which they are presented. The blocks are depicted in the second column. The next column, which is headed 11, shows the correct response for each block. The other figures show the incorrect responses receiving partial credit; each is placed in the column that designates the number of points it receives. Since the child is allowed three trials on each block if he cares to take them, all trials are recorded on the blank by writing the figures 1, 2, or 3 on the diagram of the response made if it is a credited error, or in the proper column if it is a correct response. Error responses for which no credit points are indicated are entered in column 1. Since only the *last* response is scored it is essential that each reaction made by the child be recorded on the scoring sheet by the numerals 1, 2, or 3, so that it will be absolutely clear which response was final.

A lightweight clip board is provided for holding the scoring sheet during the test, so that it may lie in the examiner's lap and the recording of responses may remain unnoticed by the subject. A very short pencil with rubber tip is best for recording responses, because it can be kept between the fingers continually without interfering with the handling of other material and without attracting the child's attention. Two or more should always be at hand to avoid interruption of the test.

*Other materials.*—The blocks for Form B are identical with those for Form A except that B11 represents a small cube on its side. The blocks and objects are conveniently arranged in three boxes with covers that serve as additional trays, and there is a display board to facilitate uniformity of spacing in presenting the objects and to prevent them from undue rolling about. This display board may be laid on a chair, a couch, or a box if no low table is available and thus is valuable in giving the test in the child's own environment. An interesting book to occupy the companion's attention should also be included with the celluloid duck, the small iron truck, and the tiny jointed doll, all of which are used for preliminary play with the child. All of the materials are packed into a small case, which may serve as a low seat for the examiner in case of need. There is also a small folding seat for the child's use if there is no chair available. The main object should be to put the child completely at ease while keeping him seated in proper relationship to the material. He cannot give his full attention to the problem if he is perched on a high chair. He must be able to look down upon the blocks at a comfortable angle.

## SPECIFIC DIRECTIONS FOR GIVING AND SCORING

Very detailed directions for administering the O-F Test are given, because when no language is used an apparently slight change in the examiner's behavior may materially influence the child's reaction. Action and facial expression are substituted for language in this test, and a change in these would be as serious as omitting or elaborating the verbal directions in a language test.

Preliminary practice is very necessary to a smooth and rapid manipulation of the material and sustained interest on the part of the child. No examiner should attempt an actual test until she can almost automatically go through all the shifting of blocks and objects and the recording of responses. Anything less than this is unfair to the child.

1. *Preliminary arrangements.* — Both child and examiner should be seated upon low chairs before a low table with the child at the examiner's left and the trays of material at her right (see Plate VIII, page 70). These trays should be in order as numbered, and the material should be arranged as follows:

TRAY 1: toys for preliminary play; objects for fore-exercise; objects for series I; objects for series II.

TRAY 2: blocks for fore-exercise; blocks for series I and II.

TRAY 3: objects for series III.

TRAY 4: objects for series IV.

TRAY 5: blocks for series III and IV.

TRAY 6: objects for series V covered by block 15 inverted.

Automatic control of the material is facilitated by always returning material to the same place in the tray and by keeping used blocks tipped forward and unused blocks tipped backward in the trays.

In front of the child should be the display board with the small truck, the duck, and the doll upon it. The mother or other companion, if present, should be seated behind the child at some little distance and should be strictly cautioned against speaking, laughing, or in any way attracting the child's attention to herself. Her presence is ordinarily desirable with the younger children, as it tends to put them much more at ease in a new situation. With an extremely timid or young subject a self-controlled mother can even hold the child upon her lap and the display board in her hands without vitiating the test. In the usual examination, however, she should at this time be filling out the information blank or reading a book. Older children and children who are not timid will do better alone with the examiner.

2. *Advantages of the arrangement.*—a. The child is not made self-conscious by finding the examiner directly facing him.

b. The examiner can see the child's face and note his every reaction and yet reach behind him when necessary to adjust his chair or in other ways make him comfortable.

c. The materials can be kept at the right end of the table entirely out of reach of the child but within view, so as to arouse his curiosity.

d. The examiner's record blank is also at the right and not noticeable to the child.

e. The examiner can use both hands freely to handle the material or to control the child.

f. When an observer is present she can follow the general course of the examination but cannot dictate responses. If the child misses her, he can turn and reassure himself, but otherwise can be totally unconscious of her presence. Since the examiner faces the companion, she can, if necessary, silently remind her not to disturb.

3. *General directions as to the use of speech with children who speak and understand English.*—a. Never give any oral clue as to what is to be done or what choice is to be made, e. g., do not say, "Put something in."

b. During the actual test make as little conversation as possible.

c. If the child asks, "Which one shall I put in?" and insists on a reply, say, "Whatever one you want to." If he says, "I don't know which one," reply "Oh, I think you can tell." If he then refuses to make a choice, say, "Shall we have another one?" and change to the next block if he does not make a choice at once. Very rarely a child will desire to make or change a response after the block has been lifted from the table, but this should be allowed if he has not already used his three trials. If he has, smile and get his attention to the next block or object.

d. There is no objection to casual conversation in reply to the child's comments, but the best rule is to talk as little as possible without making the situation seem artificial to the child. Many children are so interested in the test material that they go straight through without a word; others make comments that require no reply; and a few ask direct questions. A noncommittal reply or comment, however, such as, "What do you think?" "You may do whatever you want to," usually satisfies even those who ask direct questions. In case the test is being used for comparisons between English-speaking and non-English-speaking children, the examiner should of course maintain perfect silence throughout all tests. The slight artificiality of such a situation to the talkative child is better than the confusion caused in a foreign child by a strange language. If both types of children are met with sympathetic silence, conditions are more nearly equalized.

4. *The fore-exercise.*— a. The child should be encouraged to play with the toys — to give the doll and the duck rides in turn and to attempt to negotiate the "bump" from the surface of the display board to the table and back without an accident. Free play and laughter at this time are of decided advantage in establishing friendly relations. Even a child who does not speak or understand English soon overcomes his shyness and feels at home. When it seems evident that the child is at ease, take advantage of the next accident and proceed to the next step by removing the car to the "garage" for "repairs."

b. Present the swan and the top, and while the child is examining them quietly remove the other toys and get out the first practice block (swan). Move it in front of the child's eyes so as to excite his curiosity, and quickly place the top and the swan in position at the side of the board farthest from the child, the top standing on its large end at the right and the swan facing to the right. Place the block before the child, slowly pick up the swan, turn it on its side, and fit it into place.

c. Then act much pleased, pick up the block containing the swan, display it proudly to the child, transfer it to the left hand and with the right hand place practice block 2 (top) in position with the point of the top away from the child.

d. Motion for the child to fit the top into place. If he does not attempt to do so, give the top to him and put your finger into the depression in the block. Keep trying (without a word) to get him to make the insertion, and help him gently if he needs it. With some young children it is even necessary to take their hands and go through the motion of insertion with them. Others comprehend at once and place the top. If they leave it standing on end in the block, point to the part of the recess not filled, and if the child does not make the correction slowly push the point of the top down into place. Then display both filled blocks before him for his admiration, showing your own by your attitude and facial expression.

Quickly remove the two objects from the blocks and place them in position on the display board. Set the swan block before the child, point to the objects with a sweeping motion of your hand that does not designate either one and point to the block, inserting your finger in the recess to indicate that you expect the child to choose and make an insertion. Try this two or three times before pointing to the swan, placing it in the child's hand, or otherwise helping him. If necessary, repeat step c.

e. When the child attempts to fit in an incorrect object, allow him to do so for a moment. Then point to the correct object. Get him to make the change himself if possible; if he does not, remove the incorrect object and point to the correct one, placing the latter in his hand if necessary and assisting him to insert it. *At all times give only a minimum of assistance and strive to make the child feel that he did all himself.*

f. As soon as the swan is correctly placed, display the filled block, replace the swan beside the top, and present practice block 2 (top) again, repeating only as much of the procedure in step d as is absolutely necessary.

g. Replace the objects and present each block in turn once more, striving to get the child to make the responses unaided and encouraging him to think he has done so even when you have had to help.

h. With a very distractable child who has made *no* mistake in placing objects during the second trial it is allowable to omit the third rather than to lose rapport.

5. *Series I.* — a. Taking the ball and the large box in your left hand, place them before the child while you quickly remove the fore-exercise material with your right and replace it in the tray. Keep your left hand spread over the ball and the box to prevent the child's taking them up while you secure block 1 (ball) with your right. (If the child is so insistent on having one of these new objects that his good temper is in danger of being lost, allow him to examine them a bit, then replace them, and proceed.)

b. Place block 1 in front of the child, point as before to the objects and the block, and reward the placing of the correct object by a display of the filled block. If an incorrect choice or an incorrect placing is made, show no disappointment unless the child himself does so and *give no help*. Record each of the first three placings upon the blank by numbers 1, 2, 3, below the appropriate design if an error and in the margin if correct. If the child makes an incorrect placing but appears satisfied therewith, remove the object and replace it on the display board with the left hand while securing block 2 with the right. Do not urge three trials if the child is satisfied with one or two. Remove block 1 with your left hand while attracting the child's attention to block 2, held *back* toward him to excite his curiosity. Then place block 2 and proceed as above.

6. *Series II.* — Grasp all objects for this series in the

left hand (pencil and small box resting in bowl) and place them in a group before the child, allowing him to handle them while you remove the objects of series I. Arrange these new objects in position as follows, from the child's left to right: spool (on end), pencil (pointing toward him), box (length vertical to him), bowl (right side up). Proceed with blocks 3, 4, 5, and 6, as usual, always attracting the child's attention to a new block, *before* placing it.

7. *Series III.* — Place the large cup containing the cylinder and the long block before the child first, remove the objects of series II, and place the small cup containing the square block in front of him. Then arrange the objects in the following order from left to right: large flaring cup (handle to right), square block (on side), cylinder (on base), long block (length vertical to child), small cup (handle to right). Proceed with blocks 8, 9, and 10.

8. *Series IV.* — Place all objects except the small top before the child at once, remove the objects of series III, and place the small top. Arrange the objects in the following order from left to right: large cube, large top, salt shaker, small top, small cube. Present blocks 11, 12, and 13.

9. *Series V.* — Place all the spools before the child at once; remove the objects of series IV. Arrange the spools in the following order from left to right: spool 18, spool 20, spool 19, spool 16, spool 15, spool 17. (Spool 20 is the smallest. The others are numbered in order of size, 19 being the largest. Spools 15, 16, 17, and 18 fit the block.) When the child has made eight placements, remove the block instantly *without* displaying it. Replace the truck, the doll, and the duck and allow the child to play a few moments before dismissing him.

10. *Scoring the test.* — Look over the entire sheet and encircle the number representing the *last* response to each block. On most of the blocks this will be a 3 or a 2. On block 15 this is the highest number appearing in each of the four *horizontal* rows; in a C (correct) or G (graded)

response to block 15 the encircled numbers lie in a straight line from the upper left to the lower right of the diagram. In an A response (attempt at adjustment) this line must be straight through three consecutive levels unless there are seven trials. Circle the letter representing the credit allowed for block 15. (See Chapter III, page 53, for credit given to each response.) Enter the credits allowed for each block in the column at the extreme right. Add the credits for all encircled responses. This is the child's point score, called the O-F score, which should be used in making any matched-group comparisons. His relative mental ability as compared with children of his own age may be found by reference to the decile values in Table XIX, page 56.

The approximate mental age corresponding to each score is found on the next page. An intelligence quotient may be estimated in the usual way by dividing the number of months of mental age by the number of months of chronological age.

11. *Form B.* — The method with Form B is exactly the same as with Form A except that each block is turned 90 or 180 degrees, as shown on the scoring sheet, and the order of blocks 9 and 10 is changed. Turn block 15 so that the largest recess is nearest the child and the smallest is farthest from him. This difference in manner of presentation effectually prevents the use of the same motor reactions for success and yet leaves the mental problem very similar in the two forms. Blocks A11 and B11 differ only in the size of the cube represented, but this necessitates the choice of a different object. Whenever possible, both forms of the test should be given (Form A *first*), and the average of the two results should be used as the child's O-F score.

### DERIVATION OF NORMS

The results from the six hundred examinations upon which the Object-Fitting Test was standardized and the method of deriving the norms may be found in Chapter III.

## TABLE XXV

### Mental Age in Months Corresponding to Each Object-Fitting Score

| O-F Score | MA | O-F Score | MA | O-F Score | MA | O-F Score | MA |
|---|---|---|---|---|---|---|---|
| 0 | 15 | 33 | 26 | 66 | 39 | 100 | 53 |
| 1 | 15 | 34 | 27 | 67 | 40 | 101 | 54 |
| 2 | 15 | 35 | 27 | 68 | 40 | 102 | 55 |
| 3 | 16 | 36 | 27 | 69 | 41 | 103 | 55 |
| 4 | 16 | 37 | 28 | 70 | 41 | 104 | 56 |
| 5 | 17 | 38 | 28 | 71 | 41 | 105 | 56 |
| 6 | 17 | 39 | 29 | 72 | 42 | 106 | 57 |
| 7 | 18 | | | 73 | 42 | 107 | 58 |
| 8 | 18 | 40 | 29 | 74 | 42 | 108 | 59 |
| 9 | 18 | 41 | 29 | 75 | 43 | 109 | 59 |
| | | 42 | 30 | 76 | 43 | | |
| 10 | 19 | 43 | 30 | 77 | 43 | 110 | 60 |
| 11 | 19 | 44 | 30 | 78 | 44 | 111 | 60 |
| 12 | 19 | 45 | 31 | 79 | 44 | 112 | 61 |
| 13 | 20 | 46 | 31 | | | 113 | 62 |
| 14 | 20 | 47 | 31 | 80 | 44 | 114 | 62 |
| 15 | 20 | 48 | 32 | 81 | 45 | 115 | 63 |
| 16 | 21 | 49 | 32 | 82 | 45 | 116 | 64 |
| 17 | 21 | | | 83 | 45 | 117 | 65 |
| 18 | 21 | 50 | 33 | 84 | 46 | 118 | 66 |
| 19 | 22 | 51 | 33 | 85 | 46 | 119 | 66 |
| | | 52 | 33 | 86 | 46 | | |
| 20 | 22 | 53 | 34 | 87 | 47 | 120 | 67 |
| 21 | 22 | 54 | 34 | 88 | 47 | 121 | 68 |
| 22 | 23 | 55 | 34 | 89 | 47 | 122 | 68 |
| 23 | 23 | 56 | 35 | | | 123 | 69 |
| 24 | 23 | 57 | 35 | 90 | 48 | 124 | 69 |
| 25 | 24 | 58 | 36 | 91 | 48 | 125 | 70 |
| 26 | 24 | 59 | 37 | 92 | 48 | 126 | 70 |
| 27 | 24 | | | 93 | 49 | 127 | 71 |
| 28 | 25 | 60 | 37 | 94 | 49 | 128 | 71 |
| 29 | 25 | 61 | 38 | 95 | 50 | 129 | 72 |
| | | 62 | 38 | 96 | 50 | | |
| 30 | 25 | 63 | 38 | 97 | 52 | 130 | 72 |
| 31 | 26 | 64 | 39 | 98 | 52 | 131 | 73 |
| 32 | 26 | 65 | 39 | 99 | 53 | 132 | 74 |

## SUMMARY

1. This Object-Fitting Test for young children is designed for those uses for which a verbal test is unsuited.

2. The test material is simple, portable, and convenient for use in the child's own environment.

3. The specific directions for giving and scoring the test should be followed exactly.

4. The norms are based upon one hundred and fifty tests at each of the four preschool year levels.

# BIBLIOGRAPHY

1. ANDERSON, ROSE G. "A Critical Examination of Test-Scoring Methods." *Archives of Psychology*, No. 80. 1925.
2. ARTHUR, GRACE. "An Attempt to Sort Children with Specific Reading Disability from Other Non-Readers." *Journal of Applied Psychology*, 11: 251–263. 1927.
3. BRIDGES, K. M. BENHAM. "Occupational Interests of Three-Year-Old Children." *Pedagogical Seminary*, 34: 415–423. 1927.
4. BRONNER, A. F., HEALY, W., LOWE, G., AND SHIMBERG, M. *A Manual of Individual Mental Tests and Testing.* Boston: Little, Brown, & Co. 1927.
5. DEARBORN, W. F., ANDERSON, J. E., AND CHRISTIANSEN, A. O. "Formboard and Construction Tests of Mental Ability." *Journal of Educational Psychology*, 7: 445–458. 1916.
6. DEARBORN, W. F., SHÁW, EDWIN A., AND LINCOLN, E. A. *A Series of Form Board and Performance Tests of Intelligence.* Harvard Monographs in Education, Series 1, No. 4. Cambridge: The Graduate School of Education, Harvard University. 1923.
7. GESELL, ARNOLD. *The Mental Growth of the Pre-School Child.* New York: The Macmillan Co. 1925.
8. GODDARD, H. H. "The Form Board as a Measure of Intellectual Development in Children." *Training School Bulletin*, 9: 49–52. 1912.
9. GOODENOUGH, FLORENCE L. "The Reliability and Validity of the Wallin Peg Boards." *Psychological Clinic*, 16: 199–215. October, 1927.
10. ————. *The Kuhlmann-Binet Tests for Children of Preschool Age.* Minneapolis: The University of Minnesota Press. 1928.
11. HALLOWELL, DOROTHY KERN. "Mental Tests for Pre-School Children." *Psychological Clinic*, 16: 235–276. November–December, 1927.
12. HEALY, W. *The Individual Delinquent.* New York: Little, Brown, & Co. 1915.

13. HERDERSCHEE, D. "Test für taubstumme Kinder." *Z. f. ang. Ps.* 16: 40–59. 1920. (Summarized in *L'année psychologie,* 22: 549. 1920–21.)

14. HERRICK, D. S. "A Comparison of Brahmin and Panchana Children in South India with Each Other and with American Children by Means of the Goddard Formboard." *Journal of Applied Psychology,* 5: 253–260. 1921.

15. HERRING, JOHN P. "The Nature of Intelligence." *Journal of Educational Psychology,* 16: 505–522. 1925.

16. IDE, GLADYS G. "The Witmer Formboard and Cylinders as Tests for Children Two to Six Years of Age." *Psychological Clinic,* 12: 65–88. May 15, 1918.

17. JOHNSON, BUFORD J. *Mental Growth of Children.* New York: E. P. Dutton and Co. 1925.

18. KOHS, S. C. *Intelligence Measurement.* New York: The Macmillan Co. 1923.

19. KUBO, V. "The Revised and Extended Binet-Simon Tests Applied to the Japanese Children." *Pedagogical Seminary,* 29:187–194. 1922.

20. KUHLMANN, F. *A Handbook of Mental Tests.* Baltimore: Warwick & York. 1922.

21. LEVY, DAVID M., AND TULCHIN, SIMON. "The Resistance of Infants and Young Children during Mental Tests." *Journal of Experimental Psychology,* 6: 304–322; 8: 209–224. 1923, 1925.

22. LINCOLN, A. "Tentative Standards for the Lincoln Hollow Square Formboard." *Journal of Applied Psychology,* 11: 264–267. 1927.

23. LOWRY, CHARLES D. "Physiology and Psychology of the Deaf Child." Proceedings of the National Education Association, pp. 1084–1091. 1911.

24. NICE, MARGARET MORSE. "A Child Who Would Not Talk." *Pedagogical Seminary,* 30: 104–142. 1925.

25. PINTNER, RUDOLPH. "The Standardization of Knox's Cube Test." *Psychological Review,* 22: 377–401. 1915.

26. PINTNER, RUDOLPH, AND ANDERSON, MARGARET. *The Picture Completion Test.* Educational Psychology Monographs, No. 20. 1917.

27. PINTNER, RUDOLPH, AND PATERSON, D. G. "The Binet Scale and the Deaf Child." *Journal of Educational Psychology,* 6: 201–210. 1915.

28. ————. "A Class Test with Deaf Children." *Journal of Educational Psychology,* 6: 591–600. 1915.

29. ————. *A Scale of Performance Tests.* New York: D. Appleton & Co. 1917.

30. PORTEUS, S. D. "The Measurement of the Intelligence of Six Hundred and Fifty-three Children Examined by the Binet and Porteus Tests." *Journal of Educational Psychology,* 9: 13–31. 1918.

31. SMITH, M. E. *An Investigation of the Development of the Sentence and the Extent of the Vocabulary in Young Children.* University of Iowa Studies in Child Welfare, Vol. III, No. 5. 1926.

32. STUTSMAN, RACHEL. *Performance Tests for Children of Preschool Age.* Genetic Psychology Monographs, No. 1. 1926.

33. SYLVESTER, R. H. *The Form Board Test.* Psychological Monographs, No. 65. Princeton: Psychological Review Co. 1913.

34. SYMONDS, PERCIVAL M. "Factors Influencing Test Reliability." *Journal of Educational Psychology,* 19: 73–87. 1928.

35. TERMAN, L. M. *The Measurement of Intelligence.* Boston: Houghton Mifflin Co. 1916.

36. THORNDIKE, E. L. *The Measurement of Intelligence.* New York: Bureau of Publications, Teachers College, Columbia University. 1927.

37. WALLIN, J. E. W. "Norms for the Sequin Formboard Based on the Average of Three Trials." *Journal of Delinquency,* 5–6: 381–386. 1920–21.

38. ————. "The Peg Formboards." *Psychological Clinic,* 12: 40–53. April 15, 1918.

39. WOOLLEY, HELEN T., AND CLEVELAND, ELIZABETH. "Performance Tests for "Three-, Four-, and Five-Year-Old Children." *Journal of Experimental Psychology,* 6: 58–68. 1923.

40. YOUNG, H. H. "Slot Maze A." *Psychological Clinic,* 14: 73–83. May–June, 1922.

41. ————. "A Speech Clinic Case with Misconduct as a By-Product." *Journal of Applied Psychology,* 9: 371–381. 1925.

42. ————. "The Witmer Formboard." *Psychological Clinic,* 10: 93–111. June 15, 1916.

43. YOUNG, H. H. AND YOUNG, M. H. "The Witmer Formboard —First Trial Records." *Psychological Clinic,* 14: 85–91. 1923.

# INDEX